1

WINDSOR CHAIRS

by

F. GORDON ROE

Collecting, History, Belles Lettres

Victorian Furniture
English Cottage Furniture
English Period Furniture: An Introductory Guide
Old English Furniture from Tudor to Regency
Coronation Cavalcade
The Life and Times of King Edward VIII
The Bronze Cross
Britain's Birthright

Art and Biography

Henry Bright of the Norwich School
Charles Bentley, Member of the 'Old Water-Colour Society'
Dictator of the Royal Academy (Joseph Farington, R.A.)
David Cox
Sporting Prints of the 18th and early 19th Centuries
Catalogue of the Pictures and Drawings in the Collection of
Frederick John Nettlefold (with C. Reginald Grundy)
Etty and the Nude (with William Gaunt)
The Nude from Cranach to Etty and Beyond
Cox the Master
Rowlandson: The Life and Art of a British Genius
Sea Painters of Britain

Mr Pickwick addresses the Club. The most famous of all illustrations showing bow-back Windsors in use.

Windsor Chairs

F. Gordon Roe

Fellow of the Society of Antiquaries of London
Fellow of the Royal Historical Society
Sometime Editor of *The Connoisseur*

PHOENIX HOUSE LTD

LONDON

To
Aunt Blanche
(Dowager Lady Swinfen)
whose passing has not effaced
a gentle memory

PER ARDUA AD ALTA:

FORTE NON IGNAVE

Printed in Great Britain
by C. Tinling & Co. Ltd., Liverpool, London and Prescot
for Phoenix House Limited, 38 William IV Street
Charing Cross, London, W.C.2

First published 1953

Contents

Notes on the Illustrations

(Except when otherwise stated, all are English-made items)

FRONTIS. *Mr Pickwick addresses the Club.* By Robert Seymour, 1836, for *The Pickwick Papers*, by Charles Dickens: the most famous of all illustrations showing bow-back Windsors in use..

FIG. I. *Each managed to glance at him stealthily.* Plain stick-back Windsors in the 'large room' of an inn, as shown in a wood-engraving by Swain after Frederick Walker (A.R.A.), for *The Prodigal Son*, by Dutton Cook, in *Once a Week* (London; Bradbury & Evans), 19 April 1862.

FIG. II. *'He has got his discharge, by G——!'* The Chancery prisoner's death in the Fleet. Extra-illustration, by Thomas Onwhyn, originally published 1837, for *Pickwick*. Note plain stick-back Windsors of the period.

FIG. III. Venetian *sgabèllo*, c. 1560, in the Victoria and Albert Museum. Pencil sketch by Fred Roe, R.I. (1864-1947). Note how back is tenoned through tail-piece of seat.

FIG. IV. *'Brother Tadger, Sir,' said Mr Stiggins, suddenly increasing in ferocity. . . . 'you are drunk, Sir.'* Extra-illustration, by Thomas Onwhyn, originally published 1837, for *Pickwick*. Note Windsor stool in foreground.

PL. 1. Early comb-back Windsor of elm, with late seventeenth-century features, but possibly of early eighteenth-century make. Note the crown in the cresting and the 'barley-sugar' rails. The legs have been shortened. Height of chair 3ft. 6in., width of seat 2ft. ½in.
Ex coll. the late Fred Skull, High Wycombe.

PL. 2. Mutilated Windsor with unusual features. Note the finely curved arms, and the front legs with 'Spanish' feet. As there were never more than two sticks and a splat in the back, this may always have been a low chair, though the present splat and back-rail are replacements. The style suggests the second quarter of the eighteenth century.
Messrs Parker-Knoll Ltd. Photo: Council of Industrial Design.

PL. 3. Windsor of good quality and possibly of Continental origin, in style about the second quarter of the eighteenth century. Note the attenuated cabrioles, the straight outline of the back, and the shaped cresting with a carved shell (rare on Windsors) and pronounced 'ears'.
Messrs Parker-Knoll Ltd. Photo: Council of Industrial Design.

PL. 4. Early Windsor of unusual form, its back showing the influence of a 'Queen Anne' type which actually reached its peak of development some

twenty years after the Good Queen's death. The legs have been cut down, thus impairing the cabriole effect of those in front; there are signs that the chair has been painted. Mid-eighteenth century.
Messrs Parker-Knoll Ltd. Photo: Council of Industrial Design.

PL. 5. Fan-back Windsor of early type in ash with elmwood seat of rectangular formation. Note the sharp splay of the legs. There are no turned parts, members having been rounded with the spokeshave. Eighteenth century.
Messrs Parker-Knoll Ltd. Photo: Council of Industrial Design.

PL. 6. Comb- or fan-back Windsor in certain respects resembling Oliver Goldsmith's Chair in the Victoria and Albert Museum, but without the back-brace and tail-piece to the seat. (Chairs of this and kindred types are often called 'Goldsmith Chairs', a term of modern coinage.) Mid-eighteenth century.
High Wycombe Museum. Photo: Council of Industrial Design.

PL. 7. Comb-back Windsor, the arm-bow, sticks, and legs of ash, the seat of elm. The reinforcing lath up the centre of the back was added for greater strength after the chair was completed. This chair has been described as 'probably Dutch'. Latter part of the eighteenth century (*cf.* Pl. 8).
Messrs Parker-Knoll Ltd. Photo: Council of Industrial Design.

PL. 8. Comb-back Windsor of blackened wood, with primitive form of stretcher, and stick-back capped by a small cresting. The bowing of the sticks may be a local compromise between the comb- and bow-back. This chair is said to be Welsh. Despite its primitive character, it may date from no earlier than the latter part of the eighteenth century (*cf.* Pl. 7).
Mr Peter Desborough.

PLS. 9 & 10. Fan-back Windsors with comb-cresting, representing a mid-eighteenth century type, but perhaps both dating from the last quarter of the century. *Right,* is the earlier in type. *ex coll. the late Fred Skull. Left,* with a late type of splat, lacks a stick from its back-brace.
Messrs Parker-Knoll Ltd. Photos: Council of Industrial Design.

PL. 11. American Writing Chair of maple and oak, the seat and writing-board of spruce. Assigned to *c.* 1775-1800.
The Metropolitan Museum of Art, New York.

PL. 12. Elegant fan-back Windsor of the late eighteenth century, with cabriole legs and well-formed splat.
Mr G. Newitt. Photo: Council of Industrial Design.

PL. 13. Windsor Settees are scarce. This fine example of a comb-back with unpierced 'vase' splats, and cabriole front legs, has been assigned to *c.* 1760-70.
Ex coll. the late C. Reginald Grundy. Courtesy of M. Harris & Sons.

Pl. 14. American Settee, eighteenth century, 47 in. high, 39 in. wide. The black paint is a recent restoration. An instance of comb- and bow-back combination.
The Metropolitan Museum of Art, New York.

Pls. 15 & 16. American Windsors of a type combining bow- and comb-back; eighteenth century. *Left,* 43½in. high, is of oak, ash, tulip, poplar, and maple. *Right,* 44in. high, of chestnut, maple, oak, and ash, was made by A. D. Allen.
The Metropolitan Museum of Art, New York.

Pl. 17. American fan-back Windsor of pine, maple, oak, and ash; height 42in.; eighteenth century. Note the pronounced splay of the legs, and spirals on ears of cresting.
The Metropolitan Museum of Art, New York.

Pl. 18. Pennsylvania comb-back of spruce and oak, 46¼in. high. Note spirals on ears of cresting, and the turning of various members. The pronounced splay of the legs is characteristic of many American Windsors. Assigned to *c.* 1750-75.
The Metropolitan Museum of Art, New York.

Pl. 19. Roomy comb-back Windsor with simple splat, and fore- and aft- cabrioles with solid brackets. Cabriole back legs are somewhat rarely present on Windsors. Late eighteenth century (restored).
Photo: Vauxhall Motors Ltd.

Pl. 20. Plain stick-back type of Windsor 'bow', here seen to advantage in an example perhaps as early as the end of the eighteenth century. This splatless type of bow-chair was a development of the earlier plain 'stick-back' of comb- or crested type. It is still being made.
Photo: Vauxhall Motors Ltd.

Pl. 21. 'Gothick' influence is seen in the upper part of the splat of this bow-back of the second half of the eighteenth century. The lower part of the splat is a frequently-encountered type of baluster. The chair has old green paint on it.
Mr G. A. Turner. Photo: Council of Industrial Design.

Pl. 22. Slightly later than Pl. 23, this 'Gothick' Windsor shows the same design adapted for use with a bow-back. The cabriole fore-legs (joined through the seat) are finished with voided brackets—a very unusual refinement on Windsors. Second half of the eighteenth century.
Mr C. A. White. Photo: Council of Industrial Design.

Pl. 23. The 'Gothick' Windsor at its most elaborate: a fine example of so-called 'Chippendale' taste of the second half of the eighteenth century, the

cabriole front legs being brought through the seat in the most satisfactory method of junction. Modern versions of this type of chair exist.
Mr G. Newitt. Photo: Council of Industrial Design.

PL. 24. Bow-back Windsor, well-formed in all its parts, of beech with elm-wood seat. Late eighteenth century.
Messrs Parker-Knoll Ltd. Photo: Council of Industrial Design.

PL. 25. Bow-back Windsor with semi-'Gothick' splat of so-called 'Chippendale' type, and cabriole fore-legs, the turned rear legs also having pad-feet. The chair is of yew with a deeply adzed seat of elm. Late eighteenth century.
Mrs E. Goodchild. Photo: Council of Industrial Design.

PL. 26. Mahogany Windsors are rare, and some are modern. This late eighteenth-century 'bow-back' is notable for its splat which, besides its pierced work, is delicately carved with wheat-ears, husks, rosettes, a swag, and scrolling in the classical taste of the period. The diagonal cross-stretchers of the under-framing are unusual on Windsors. Exhibited Art Treasures, London, 1928.
Messrs Parker-Knoll Ltd. Photo: Council of Industrial Design.

PL. 27. Comb-back chair of slightly 'fan' type. Note the delicately pierced splat, the arm-supports, and shapely cabrioles of early type, their feet scored in a manner reminiscent of the long out-moded 'Spanish foot', in vogue about the times of William and Mary, and Anne. The chair, however, is late eighteenth-century.
Messrs Parker-Knoll Ltd. Photo: Council of Industrial Design.

PL. 28. In England, some unusually tall Windsors were made about the time of the Regency or under its influence. The splat of this late edition of fan-back displays the 'Prince of Wales' Feathers'; its outline tends towards a 'frilliness' associated with the first half of the nineteenth century; and the cresting shows a Regency type of classicism. The cow-horn and spur stretcher is used.
Photo: Vauxhall Motors Ltd.

PL. 29. Contemporaneously with the 'Feathers' type (Pls. 28, 36, 38) similar Windsors have splats pierced with *motifs* suggestive of classical urns, inverted husk-ornament, or floral forms—it is sometimes difficult to be quite sure which was intended, as the rural benchman was apt to blend the shapes. Some such devices also occur on 'lath and baluster' chairs of later date.
Photo: Vauxhall Motors Ltd.

PL. 30. Best-known of all English Windsors is the 'Wheel-splat' type of bow-back which, introduced about the late eighteenth-early nineteenth century, has been made in great numbers ever since. Minor variations of form or detail occur, wheel-splats being more familiar in lower-backed chairs

than that here figured, which may be an off-shoot of the Regency. If but seldom antiquarianly important, the wheel-splat Windsor thoroughly justifies its traditional popularity.
Photo: Vauxhall Motors Ltd.

PL. 31. The Pine Kitchen at the Henry Francis du Pont Winterthur Museum, Delaware, showing American Windsors with continuous back-and-arm bows, and turnings of 'Rhode Island' type. *Rear Left:* A Windsor low-back settee of eighteenth-century type, with carved knuckles to the arms.
Courtesy of the Henry Francis du Pont Winterthur Museum. Photo: Gottscho-Schleisner.

PL. 32. 'Interlaced Bow', a 'Gothick' type of Windsor originating in the late eighteenth-early nineteenth century, or under Regency influence. The type was continued to a much later date, and has undergone a limited revival in modern times. The example seen here was made *c.* 1910. Its back is of bent ash.
Mr T. C. Sutton. Photo: Council of Industrial Design.

PL. 33. Related to the 'Interlaced Bow' (Pl. 32) and originating in a like period is this attractive late-type, bow-back Windsor. The excellent example illustrated, its back supported by a nice arrangement of bent-ash stays, was framed as late as *c.* 1910.
Mr W. Hands. Photo: Council of Industrial Design.

PL. 34. Triple-splat Windsor showing so-called 'Hepplewhite' influence, the bow of yew. Note the turned bosses on the splats, a latish alternative to the 'wheel'. Old triple-splat Windsors are usually of nineteenth-century date; this example has been assigned to *c.* 1840.
Mr L. H. Collins. Photo: Council of Industrial Design.

PL. 35. Simple fan-back Windsor with undished circular seat. Descendant of a mid-eighteenth century type, of which quite modern examples are found. In the present instance the turning of the legs is of a pattern popular in the early nineteenth century and later.
Photo: Council of Industrial Design.

PL. 36. a & b. Children's High Chairs of types belonging to the earlier part of the nineteenth century. *Left*, 'Cross' variety of 'wheel-splat'; *Right*, 'Prince of Wales' Feathers' type of Regency origin. The latter has formerly had a foot-rest.
Mrs C. Skull (left); Mrs A. M. Crawley (right). Photo: Council of Industrial Design.

PL. 37. Elegant bow-back Windsor with triple-splat formation and unusually neat finish of the arm-tops and bases of arm-supports. A design of Regency ('Hepplewhite') origin.
Mr T. C. Sutton. Photo: Council of Industrial Design.

PL. 38. Unusual triple-splat Windsor of 'Prince of Wales' Feathers' type, the device being repeated in the small side-splats supporting the arms. The plumes are enriched with applied turned buttons, and the underframing has a cow-horn and spur stretcher.
Mr G. Newitt. Photo: Council of Industrial Design.

PLS. 39 & 40. Bow-back Windsors of 'Yorkshire' or 'Lancashire' type. They represent a style which spilled over from the close of the eighteenth century and flowed well on into the nineteenth, being progressively associated with a 'woolly' type of splat and heavy turnings as it approached the mid-century.
Miss I. Donald. Photos: Council of Industrial Design.

PL. 41. 'Mendlesham Chair', by Daniel and Richard Day, of Mendlesham, Suffolk. Early nineteenth century; a stylish example of the East Anglian version of the Windsor. Richard Day is said to have been at one time with Thomas Sheraton. A similar chair is in Christchurch Mansion, Ipswich.
Mr T. C. Sutton. Photo: Council of Industrial Design.

PL. 42. 'Tablet-top' Windsor of Regency style, but assigned to *c.* 1840. Given to High Wycombe Museum by Mr J. R. Myrton.
Photo: Council of Industrial Design.

PL. 43. 'Lath and Baluster' Windsor of beech with elm seat, and double cross-stretcher—a feature somewhat favoured at the period (*cf.* Pl. 47). Chairs of this and allied types are of nineteenth-century origin, this example suggesting a date somewhere about the mid-century.
Mr J. W. Wright. Photo: Council of Industrial Design.

PLS. 44 & 45. Two of many varieties of 'Scroll' Windsors which carried the 'Regency' tradition well into the nineteenth century. Though sometimes assigned to the latter part of the eighteenth century, such chairs are mostly much later in date, old examples often approximating to the middle third of the nineteenth century. *Left, Mr W. Gardner. Right, Mr T. Bristow.*
Photos: Council of Industrial Design.

PL. 46. Red-stained 'Smoker's Bow' in a style of about the mid-nineteenth century and with more elegant turnery than appears on later examples. The back edge of the seat is impressed with 'DH' in a kidney-shaped compartment. From Princes Risborough, Bucks, and doubtless of Wycombe make.
Dr J. B. C. Grundy. From English Cottage Furniture (Phoenix House Ltd.).

PL. 47. Berger (*bergère*) Bow Windsor, with shaped back and arms in three pieces. Seemingly stamped 'DG 163' on back-edge of seat, and probably by Daniel Glenister & Son, High Wycombe, *c.* 1850-65.
Dr J. B. C. Grundy. From English Cottage Furniture (Phoenix House Ltd.).

PL. 48. Besides chairs and, less commonly, settees, Windsor stools are found, in both three-legged and four-legged types. Antique examples are rare. Despite its superficially primitive appearance, the example illustrated has been assigned to *c.* 1870, and the turning is of late pattern. The stool is painted black.

High Wycombe Museum. Photo: Council of Industrial Design.

Pl. 49. a & b. *Left,* 'Gothic Spindle' Windsor, with turned spindles in the back, of a type originating in the first half of the nineteenth century, and still in production after 1865. *Mr S. G. Fane. Right,* the commonest of all the many types of 'Scroll' Windsor, of beech with elm seat. Though the design is of 'Regency' origin, such chairs continued to be made in large numbers during the latter half of the nineteenth century and later. *Mrs A. M. Crawley. Photo: Council of Industrial Design.*

Pl. 50. Wycombe lath-back Windsor in beech, stained red and varnished to imitate rose-wood or mahogany. Though mid-nineteenth century in style, this chair was framed at the end of the century, or at the beginning of the twentieth.

High Wycombe Museum. Photo: Council of Industrial Design.

Pl. 51. Typical Wycombe lath-and-baluster Windsor in beech, stained red and varnished. Such chairs were made in quantity over an extensive period in the nineteenth century, the turnings on this example being of a type favoured from about the mid-century. Note the splat directly descended from an eighteenth-century design.

Mrs W. Cooke. Photo: Council of Industrial Design.

Pl. 52. A 'Goodchild Windsor', by H. E. ('Jack') Goodchild (1885-1950), of Naphill, near High Wycombe, Bucks. Though a relatively simple instance of his work, this 'wheel-back' of beech with elm seat has been selected as showing with what distinction a traditional design can be interpreted by a master-craftsman. For comparative purposes, this example is shown 'in the wood' (or 'in the white'), *i.e.* unstained and unpolished.

Photo: Council of Industrial Design.

Pl. 53. The traditional background: interior of 'Jack' Goodchild's workshop at Naphill, Bucks, with Windsors in various stages of manufacture. Note (*centre*) a rack for keeping bows in good shape.

Photo: C. E. Sweetland, A.R.P.S.

Pl. 54. 'Jack' (Harold Edward) Goodchild (1885-1950) filing a Gothick splat in his workshop at Naphill, Bucks.

Photo: C. E. Sweetland, A.R.P.S.

PROEM

Even so homely a theme as the Windsor Chair has its complexities. Compact of myth and history, of tradition and change, it leads us into relatively uncharted regions through which this book essays to blaze a clearer trail for the benefit of such as may follow after. For the most part, Windsors, despite their popularity, are dealt with as a pleasing by-way in the crafts, and, though accounts of them in general works on furniture are sometimes valuable, there is yet room for a more intensive study of these chairs which everybody knows and likes—and too readily takes for granted. Even now, it is possibly true to suggest that, as collectors' pieces, Windsors are rather more seriously studied in America than in England, where, on the whole, it is the deeply-rooted *tradition* of these chairs that has the most general appeal. The fact of being a Windsor Chair endows such pieces, old or new, with a vague distinction, none the less effective because it is in essence affectionate.

Primarily, this book is about English Windsors, though a chapter on the American-made varieties is essential to any consideration of the subject as a whole. That American Windsors are here dealt with in less detail than the English is no derogation of their interest or importance. It is, for instance, obvious that quite a number of details of method and construction are shared by both, and, in starting (as, in my opinion, I have properly done) from the English end of the stick, there is the less reason to indulge in repetitions. It is, however, fair to warn the average reader (whom, in Chestertonian phrase, I believe to exist) that Windsors, whenever made, are not a subject on which definition can be expected at every point. If the general trend of their development is known, many obscurities remain—and, as far as my own knowledge goes, are likely to remain—though doubtless not a few 'loose ends' will be neatly tied together by skilled observers in the light of newly discovered evidence or of fresh deduction.

Such, then, is the tenor of this book, though it remains for me to express my gratitude to all who have helped me, whether by the printed word or by direct assistance. It is impossible to list every book or article concerning Windsors, though a useful selection of those consulted is acknowledged in the Notes and Short Bibliography.

On the personal side I wish especially to thank Mr L. John Mayes, F.L.A., Borough Librarian of High Wycombe, for useful information and suggestions. To Alderman R. A. Janes (Director, Messrs Nicholls & Janes Ltd), I am much indebted for his ready response to my inquiries, and for courteously permitting me to draw upon his written reminiscences, some extracts from which appeared in *The Cabinet Maker*, 4 August, 1951, but which I have been enabled to consult in their original form. Mr T. C. Parker (Chairman, Messrs Parker-Knoll Ltd) has generously devoted much time to discussing with me the remarkable collection of antique chairs preserved at the Parker-Knoll Factory for the inspiration and instruction of its employees. Mr F. H. Glenister and Mr W. R. Butler (Messrs Thomas Glenister Ltd) have been of much assistance in affording me information about the history of their firm and thus clearing up some datal problems. Valuable aid has been given by Mr A. B. R. Fairclough, Photographic Librarian of the Council of Industrial Design, and his staff. Among others who have helped are my wife (with a valuable suggestion); the Rev. D. J. Amies, Vicar of Great Marlow, Bucks; Mr M. C. Bird (High Wycombe Public Library); Mr Cyril G. E. Bunt, Drawings Curator, Royal Institute of British Architects; Mr Adrian Bury, Hon. R.W.S.; Mr Desmond Butler; Mr Peter Desborough; Mrs E. Goodchild (for information about her late husband, Mr 'Jack' Goodchild); Mr Edwin Gunn; the Rev. A. L. Evan Hopkins, M.A., Vicar of High Wycombe; Mr Thomas Mackenzie, C.A.; Mr Charles F. Montgomery, Executive Secretary and Associate Curator, Henry Francis Du Pont Winterthur Museum, Delaware; Miss Cecelia Neville (but for whom I should have missed a necessary quotation); the Society of Genealogists; Messrs Vauxhall Motors Ltd; Miss Alice Winchester, Editor of The Magazine *Antiques*, New York; and, as always, the Staffs of the Libraries of the British Museum and the Victoria and Albert Museum; also the Metropolitan Museum of Art, New York, and all other owners of Windsors herein illustrated, and whose names I have endeavoured to note elsewhere in this book.

In every instance the copyright of an illustration is vested in the owner or owners thereof. Should any acknowledgment have been omitted, I proffer apology for an inadvertence. Photographs accredited to the Council of Industrial Design are the copyright of that body, and sundry ownerships of chairs are given as entered in its records.

I desire also specially to thank Mr Douglas W. Bryant, Director of Libraries, American Embassy, London; Dr Jane de Iongh, Cultural

Attaché, Royal Netherlands Embassy, London; and Mr Th. H. Lunsingh Scheurleer, Curator of the Rijksmuseum, Amsterdam, for courteous replies to my inquiries.

57 Peel Street,   F. GORDON ROE
Kensington, W.8.

CHAPTER I

The Mythos

I

LIFE is ripe with rumour. It is—at any rate, has been—no uncommon thing for families to grace their rise in the social scale by developing traditions more than hinting at a bygone stateliness or a long antiquity of race. Not all such traditions (so to style them) have a factual basis, however innocent their declaration. A high percentage of the vaguer tales, as well as some of the more detailed, have become traditional merely by force of repetition. Better it were to call them theories, thus separating them from such true traditions as have survived, and from pedigrees properly reconstructed on scientific principles. Misunderstanding, aimless guess-work, coupled with a natural disposition to multiply two by two with the aim of making forty accounts for a large proportion of alleged traditions, even when conscious forgery is not in question.

What is true of families or persons is in some sense true of furniture. As with genealogy and the more romantic aspects of ethnography, furniture-studies abound in speculative matter, in process of sifting by competent authorities who, despite much patient research, have yet to grapple with and vanquish a gaudy horde of guesses. A fair example of this need to ungild the lily is provided by the Windsor Chair, the setting of which has become so thickly overgrown with more or less imaginative guesses. Be it said at once that most of this specialized mythology is of modern incidence, nourished by the rapid growth of interest in a peculiarly attractive form of traditional seating.

Time was, not long ago, when Windsors were of but small account. Seldom more than what would now be called 'utility' chairs for use in modest settings, their declination in the social scale had become so marked that one scarcely looked to find them elsewhere than in the kitchen, pub, or schoolroom, or such other places where cheap, hard-wearing chairs were desirable. Granted that, with certain exceptions to be noted as they arise, the Windsor's English *milieu* had almost always been that of the servants' hall rather than the reception room, of the lesser middle-class dwelling, the cottage, or the counting-house, than of the modish apartment, the fact remains that Windsors had given ground before the massed onset of mahogany and horsehair. If scarce, enough superior Windsors have survived to point the moral that not all of them were made for the humblest usage. A limited aristocracy of Windsors suggests a propriety of use in some such settings as the butler's pantry, the more opulent type of farmhouse, or the homes of the better *bourgeoisie*. Indeed, a few may have graced still 'better' backgrounds, as certainly happened at a late stage of their history.

Fig. I. Plain stick-back Windsors in the 'large room' of an inn, as shown in a wood-engraving by Swain after Frederick Walker (A.R.A.).

Even so, the normal *milieu* of the Windsor remained constant, as any-one can see by comparing the inn-scenes of Robert Seymour's famous plate *Mr Pickwick addresses the Club* (1836) with one designed by Frederick Walker (afterwards A.R.A.) for Dutton Cook's *The Prodigal Son* in *Once a Week* (1862) (*Frontis.* and Text Fig. I). Though utterly

different in other respects, both illustrations show bow-back Windsors
in actual use. Various instances of Windsors in the original illustrations
or extra-illustrations of Dickens's books could be adduced, invariably
in poor or lower middle-class environments (Text Fig. II). The presence
of Windsors in London parks up to somewhere about the mid-1890's
(as Mr Symonds has told us) perpetuated yet another popular usage of
such chairs: a usage harking back to their employment in old tea-gardens
and such early pleasure-resorts as Ranelagh or Vauxhall. True, a somewhat limited renascence of polite interest occurred under aesthetic and
antiquarian influences towards the close of the nineteenth century. Stick-
back Windsors of, or emulating, the so-called 'Goldsmith' type are shown
'In a London Drawing Room' as drawn by A. Jule Goodman to illustrate
a playlet in the first volume of *Pearson's Magazine* (1896). And Volume
I of *The Studio* (1893) gives us a glimpse of a 'Dining Room at Harring-
ton Gardens', in one of the newer and more artistic South Kensington
houses, designed by George and Peto, and part-furnished with antiques
—among them an old bow-back Windsor with the so-called 'cow-horn'
stretcher. Such technicalities as 'cow-horn', 'bow-back' and the like will
be explained in due course; the point now made is that, in the 'naughty
nineties', there were those 'aware of art' and aware of Windsors, though
to the mass of the people such things remained merely useful, common,
and in no wise remarkable, though likable, and held in that semi-affection-
ate disregard which we bestow on familiar objects; but craftsmen there
were and had been who saw them as craftsmen's work. When, back in
1885, William Morris 'found himself the moving force of the "Socialist
League" ', he 'had to pay for the rooms and the Windsor chairs to furnish
them'.[1] As craftwork of the people, they stood for Morris's particular
brand of democracy. Also they were undeniably cheap, strong, and convenient. Save here and there, not yet had antique Windsors won their way
to connoisseurdom.

When, in my own boyhood, I discovered a brace of old 'wheel-splat'
Windsors in the kitchen of my maternal grandparents' house at Putney,
I had visual proof of the disregard of items which, if in this instance plain
and ordinary, were none the less antique. Be it stressed that my good
grandsire was architect, artist, and connoisseur. But those particular
chairs were not of consequence to him. Old, they certainly were—but
that was all. You could buy their modern fellows any day—and so, indeed,
you could, and can. Of his kindliness, he gave those chairs to me for my
'museum'. My daughter has them yet.

Thus it was in the early years of the twentieth century that I found my first Windsors, since when the situation has changed out of recognition. Slowly, but in the long run surely, antique Windsors became collectable. Slowly but surely, they achieved a status far beyond what most of them had ever known. It was realized by collectors that these disregarded chairs were useful, sightly, even elegant, and that they had an uncommon knack of 'going with' other antiques. While the cottage, tea-garden, and such-like places continued to use Windsors, the Great House and the Mansion began to find an honoured place for them, and prices rose accordingly. It became apparent to the collector that all Windsors were not out of the same stable. There were Windsors *and* Windsors, the finest old examples reaching prices which would have driven their makers (long since gone to their anonymous account) stark, staring mad. Even, be it whispered, fakes came into being, or at any rate chairs which were somewhat more than merely traditional exploitations of long-existent styles. One has heard tales of single antique Windsors mysteriously blossoming into whole sets, and there are Windsors, generally of unusual and impressive character, which, for whatever purpose they were made in the first place, have somehow graduated as the sort of 'antiques' which are given a wide berth by the cautious student. Though imitation may be indulged for other reasons than monetary gain, it is mainly for gain that false antiques are loosed upon the collecting world.

Necessarily this somewhat commercial apotheosis stimulated inquiry into the origin and history of such kindly, unassuming household gods. Authoritative experts began to pay them critical attention. It was not the fault of such authorities that the 'Windsor' mythos begat a bastard brood of legend; rather it was their purpose to check such idle spawning and to treat the Windsor Chair with the same respect as that devoted to any other worthwhile study.

That the study *is* worth while is now obvious to anyone who has felt the charm of Windsors. Of the English traditional types of chair, the Windsor is probably the most popular, while in America its rediscovery has awakened an ever-growing enthusiasm. Though scholarly investigation of the Windsor's history is still in progress, if much concerning it has yet to be discovered, enough is known to warrant discussion of a class of furniture which arouses love as well as interest in a sympathetic owner.

Before going further, it will be as well to remind the reader of the stories told, and the theories advanced, anent the rise of Windsors: stories, in some instances, as unreliably picturesque as any family pseudo-tradition.

Fig. II. Extra-illustration, by Thomas Onwhyn, originally
published 1837, for *Pickwick*.

II

Exactly why Windsors were so called is as debatable as their origin. The
name is not peculiar to all forms of Windsor. Mr Symonds has warned us
that in Somerset such chairs are known as 'stick-backs' only, and this,
now freely applied in the sub-classification of Windsors, may well have
been the older title. Again, 'Scole' and 'Mendlesham' Chairs, though of
Windsor genus, are known by their East Anglian names, as will appear
in Chapter III. Not improbably J. C. Loudon's description (1833) of the
Windsor, as 'one of the best kitchen chairs in general use in the midland

counties of England',* gives some indication of the original disposition
of a name now freely applied to all but a handful of strongly localized
varieties. That the term was somewhat less widespread in the 1860's
might seem to be suggested by a passage in the fourth chapter of Anthony
Trollope's *The Last Chronicle of Barset* (1866-67). Describing the un-
fortunate Mr Crawley's house at Hogglestock, Trollope speaks of the
'wretched, poverty-stricken room', with its one armchair, 'a Windsor-
chair as such used to be called, made soft by an old cushion in the back',
and, true to the text, two of George H. Thomas's excellent plates to the
book show this chair as a plain stick-back bow of the commonest sort.

All the same, counter-evidence shows that the name was not then
extinct, and Dickens, whose world was wider than Trollope's, made no
bones about calling a Windsor a Windsor, when it suited his purpose.
There is that allusion to an old lady 'in a clean cap and a Windsor armchair', seated outside her door at the 'Almshouses of the Cork-Cutters'
Company', in Dickens's *Somebody's Luggage*, published as the Christmas
number of *All the Year Round* for 1862; and this, coupled with divers
trade references of the same period, shows that the name of 'Windsor'
had endured, though how it arose in the first place is another matter.

There would seem to be no good reason especially to relate Windsors
to the royal and ancient town of Windsor in Berkshire, and, though such
chairs were made in various parts of England, one of their main centres
of manufacture was (and is) well away in the adjoining county of Bucking-
ham. Had the name survived as Wycombe, instead of Windsor, it would
have been easily explicable. Indeed, 'Wycombe Chair' demonstrably
covered Windsor types, as well as others not of the Windsor genus, and
thus is not sufficiently definitive. That Windsors were made at Windsor
itself, or in the neighbourhood thereof, is possible, though probably not
to any such extent as at High Wycombe. Among attempts to account
for this anomaly, we meet a tale as popular as it is, alas!, untrustworthy.

This pleasing anecdote, 'largely current in America',[2] relates how
George III, caught abroad in a shower of rain near Windsor Castle,
took shelter in a cottage, where he was accommodated with a chair which
took his fancy. Hence Windsor Chair! Admittedly 'Farmer George' had
a kindly taste for dropping in on his humbler subjects. Be it noted, too,
that the allusion is clearly to the bestowal of a name on an already existent
type of chair, which would serve well enough were it not plain that both
chair and name are older than the tradition.

Thus, though his amiable and Most Sacred Majesty may well have used

* See Appendix.

and approved Windsor Chairs—maybe on more than one occasion—
there would seem to be no more particular reason to connect him with
their history. Nor, for that matter, His Majesty's great-grandfather, King
George I, whose less agreeable memory has been also dragged into the
mythology of Windsors, perhaps as a concession to greater datal probability. A story, variously attributed to George I and George II, would
have us believe that the monarch, seeing and liking some such chair at
a chairmaker's, ordered a supply for use at Windsor Castle, though here
again (as Mr Symonds warned us in 1935) the tale remains unproven.
At least with George I and II we touch a period when a fully developed
Windsor type was demonstrably in being, and when documentary evidence for the name itself is becoming available. The earliest direct reference
to Windsors known in 1935 to Mr Symonds belongs to 1728—George
II had ascended the throne in 1727; though an unestablished allusion in
1708, when Queen Anne was reigning, was also noted. More explicit
is a London advertisement of 1730, cited in Messrs M. Harris & Sons'
useful book on *The English Chair* (1946; p. 176), and emanating from
a certain John Brown in St Paul's Churchyard: 'All sorts of Windsor
Garden Chairs, of all sizes, painted green or in the Wood'—'in the wood'
still meaning what is otherwise termed 'self-coloured'.

Yet another theory is that Windsors were so called from some un-
defined association with the ancestry of the Earls of Plymouth, (family
name now Windsor-Clive[3]). At one time, this noble race held Bradenham,
where one of them, Edward, 3rd Lord Windsor, entertained Gloriana
in 1566. Bradenham lies a few miles from the heart of High Wycombe,
famed as a chair-making centre and as a focus of the Windsor type of
chair. Hence, again, Windsor Chair.

Which is all very well, but if the tale of George III is too late in the day
for our purpose, it looks as though the Bradenham theory is too early.
The Windsor family had Bradenham from between 1500-21 till 1642,
and, though it continued in the female line of descent, it was (to quote,
G.E.C.: *Complete Peerage*) 'undoubtedly alienated before 1660'. It would
indeed be noteworthy to unearth a specific reference to Windsor Chairs,
as such, at anything like that period. One smells an antiquarian rat! If
there be any real association between the Windsor Chair and this gentle
and ennobled stock of Windsor, the likelihood would favour its having
arisen at a considerably later date.

Even so, the Bradenham theory strikes timidly by comparison with
one which, leaving the name to look after itself, gropes back for the origin
of Windsors into the darkness of the Middle Ages. That the Windsor is

a traditional type of chair is not in doubt; the problem is how far away the traditional element extends? Most of us would give it a clean bill back to Dutch William's time, or thereabouts. Was it then invented or was it evolved from something very much older? Chairs of semi- or proto-Windsor type are known, some of them attributed (rightly or wrongly) to the seventeenth century, the sixteenth century, and indeed much earlier than that. Take, as a single instance, one of the interesting survivals, a low, stick-back, three-legged chair with a rudimentary splat, in the ancient Hospital of St Cross at Winchester. One has even known this rustic piece to be attributed to the thirteenth century, when, to paraphrase an actual comment, it would have been stout enough to bear a knight in full harness! Possibly; but is the chair as old as all that? I venture to doubt so lavish an estimate of its antiquity. Roughly made and battered as it is, this chair is difficult to date precisely, though, in my opinion, the period thus assigned to it seems altogether too early—perhaps by some few hundreds of years.

There are, however, other all-wood chairs more or less suggestive of the Windsor type, some of which may well have preceded the mass of acknowledged Windsors. It thus seems possible that there is something in the theory of evolution from an earlier type, though, as generally presented, the suggestion is to me a trifle reminiscent of the reputed 'origin' of a family with which I have the honour of being distantly connected. Bear in mind that chair allegedly suitable for a knight in his mailie sark, and then listen to a tale of a house of good repute, which had enjoyed a well-earned rise to prosperity in the earlier part of the nineteenth century. The parallel is not exact, but it will serve our purpose.

This family, then; its earlier history remains obscure, but some time after its increase of fortune there arose among its members a tradition of an ancestral crusader, who (doubtless amongst other exploits) had married a Saracen woman, the which may be accounted to him for courtesy. All very interesting, but that sort of tradition has the ring of false coin. Quite likely, the story originated in the detail that the family coat-of-arms was charged with a rash of *crescents*, and *crescents* symbolized slaughtered paynims, as anyone ought to know. Hence the ancestral crusader—who in all probability never existed at all. That *crescents* by no means necessarily implied slaughtered paynims to the mediaeval mind, and that the very coat in which they so bravely figured may itself have been borrowed, was not understood by the good folk who thus bedecked their family tree with colourful trappings.

If this be an unfair comparison (as in some ways it is), it shows the ease with which, once given a fair start, a 'pedigree' can grow and flourish like the bay tree. I have said that there may be something in the claim to ancient lineage for our Windsor chairs. What is needed is more examples of indisputable proto-Windsors, before we unhesitatingly pin our faith to the Windsor's mediaeval Tree of Jesse.

III

Yet another version of the evolutionary theory of the Windsor's origin is that defined by the late Sir Lawrence Weaver.[4] Eschewing romantic implications, this simply derives the Windsor from a type of stool, as common as in principle it is ancient, with a wooden seat bored with three or four holes to take the legs. In Weaver's view, the flat top of such stools was elaborated, by shaping and hollowing, to 'saddle' shape; the next evolutionary stage being 'when the maker bored two holes in the top of the seat, bent a stick hoop-shaped, drove its ends into the two holes, and added one or two vertical spindles to make a chair-back. That', added Weaver, 'was the first "Windsor Chair", wherever it was made.'[4]

That some such progression from plain stool to Windsor Chair took place need not be doubted, and the detail that the earliest known Windsors are not hoop- or bow-backed but crested does not seriously impede the general application of the theory. What *does* remain unanswered is *when* such stools thus 'grew' a back and so became Windsor Chairs? Certainly at no recent period, on the evidence of existing examples which are found fully-fledged long after chairs in general had emerged from the box-stage on the one hand, or the legged stool on the other. In fact, the bow-back Windsor was relatively so late a development as to dismiss any idea that 'the first "Windsor Chair", wherever it was made', possessed this feature. Be it noted that here, and elsewhere in this book, 'bow-back' refers to the *elevation* of the back and not to the arm-bow, which occurs much earlier. True, some writers have assigned the advent of the bow-back to *circa* 1740, though it seems clear that most of the early examples belong to the second half of the century. That in other respects Weaver's theory is broadly acceptable must not blind us to its failure fully to suggest the protracted growth of the Windsor method. Nor is there any obvious cause to attribute the creation of the Windsor to any one place or person. As with similarities of surname, it is a fruitful source of error to assume that similarity of design *per se* implies a common source or ancestor. Not only are 'obvious' forms diffused with great rapidity, but some (it would seem) arise spontaneously in widely separated areas. That the convenient Windsor type was widely copied, adapted and transplanted at this or that stage of its history need not be doubted. Its *origin* presents another problem about which, at present, we can merely speculate. It may be conjectured with some show of confidence that however Windsors first came into being, they are, in their developed forms, as much the property of England as of any other country. In so saying, one is not ignoring America's claim to have produced some of the oldest as well as some of the most shapely 'true' Windsors to have survived the assaults of time.

IV

A point to be made at this stage arises from the distribution of the Windsor type or its approximations in divers parts of the world. Prevalent in England and America (or parts thereof), it has also had its counterparts, or its remoter relatives, in the European continent. As far afield as Tyrol are encountered low-back, corner chairs of all-wood construction[5] approximating to the English 'Smoker's Bow' or 'Smoker Bow', of which more anon (Pl. 46); and if we take in chairs not of stick-back but of wainscot type, it is not over-fanciful to detect a relationship of sorts between the Windsor and a multitude of chairs in various parts of Europe. Many of these have shaped backs, cut from a solid plank, sometimes with minor perforations. Some have stick-legs; some have fore-and-aft supports cut from the solid; but the general method of construction, with backs and supports tenoned throughout into the wooden seats, is similar to a basic principle of Windsor-technique (Text Fig. III). However grandiose it may appear to argue an affinity of sorts between a common or garden Windsor and such richly carved *sgabèlli** as the mid-to-late sixteenth-century Venetian items 5680, 5682, 5686-1859 in the Victoria and Albert Museum (to cite a mere handful of examples, of which, by the way, the seats are neatly dished), it would be foolish to close one's eyes to the possibilities thus opened up, especially when, as with 7199-1860, the back is of a fan-shape by no means unlike the outline of certain Windsors. Admittedly, this particular detail could have arisen independently, and it is scarcely within the bounds of probability that any continuity could be established.

---

* *Sgabèllo*, literally stool (or bench). Be it remembered that what is now called in English a single (as opposed to an arm-) chair was originally a 'Back-stool'.

Fig. III. Venetian *sgabèllo*, *c.* 1560, in the Victoria and Albert Museum.
[Sketch by Fred Roe, R.I.]

Apart from the minor perforations already mentioned, such continental chairs can be regarded as solid-backed, though exceptions exist, as in the case of a seventeenth-century chair of Swiss origin, 901-1904 in the Victoria and Albert Museum, of which the back resembles a couple of splats with an ornamental cresting all carved in one piece; and, for practical purposes, may be accounted as solid the unusual English chair of *circa* 1675-80, with oval back and circular seat, on scrolled front and partly-turned back legs, W.34-1918 in the Victoria and Albert Museum, to which it was given by the 7th Duke of Buccleuch. (For an illustration, see Ralph Edwards: *English Chairs*, 1951, pl. 37.) In fact, the back and seat are frames covered in leather; but though this chair from Boughton House, Northants, is not a Windsor, its construction has points in common with Windsor technique, and the way in which the base of the back is slotted right through the seat is interesting. As to what extent such a chair is a connecting link, if it be one at all, between the English Windsor and the continent is no matter for lightsome judgment.

It is, however, pertinent to ask in what degree the Windsor design was influenced from the Netherlands? Now and again, collectors, British and American, are introduced to Windsors described as 'Dutch', 'probably

Dutch', or even as 'Dutch or Belgian'. Pl. 7 is an instance. The suggestion that the Windsor chair was in some wise affected by Dutch example is not unattractive. One recalls how, in painting, the British Schools of Landscape, Sporting, and Marine Art were heavily influenced by Dutch infiltrations, still rampant just about the time that the Windsor is, beyond question, first apparent in England. One recalls how English furniture-design was itself so influenced in the second half of the seventeenth century; and one notes a correspondence between the oval back of the Boughton House chair and the small oval panels in the back of such a piece as the seventeenth-century Dutch circular armchair, 98-1891 in the Victoria and Albert Museum, though this again is not a Windsor. On the other hand, not much even distantly approaching the Windsor type is seen in Dutch paintings of the seventeenth century*; and so early a true Windsor as that in Pl. 1 exhibits 'barley-sugar' turnings of what has been defined as the English as opposed to the Dutch-Flemish twist.[6] There is no occasion to regard it as anything but an English chair.

In plain fact, there would seem to be no reliable evidence on which to base a theory that the true Windsor was of Dutch origin. Indeed, I am able to state on the authority of the Curator of the Rijksmuseum, Amsterdam (Mr Th. H. Lunsingh Scheurleer), that, so far as their present knowledge extends, 'the "Windsor Chair" is *not* Dutch', though it is probable that even in the eighteenth century some Windsors were sent from England to Holland, 'but even in that respect nothing is known with certainty'. This leaves us at liberty to draw the inference that any Windsors which may have been made in Holland trace their descent from chairs exported from England, and that a similar explanation may well account for the rise of the American Windsor.

By fairly general acceptance, the American Windsor is regarded as a development of the English product, though the relationship between both of them and the solid-back, stick-leg chairs of the European Continent remains indefinite. For what it may be worth, my present opinion of the problem is that any relationship between these and the Windsor is very roughly analogous to that as between Neanderthal Man and Neanderthaloid. In different words, and by means of an inexact parable doubtless unacceptable to Mr Gradgrind, that the one was in some sense a 'herald' of the other. Whatever were the circumstances of the Windsor's

---

* A comparison of sorts is suggested by a proto-Windsor type of low-back chair, with curved cresting holding back-sticks acutely fanned from a central upright, as pictured in the younger David Teniers' *Players at Tric-trac*, in the National Gallery, London (242). Chairs of more or less similar principle were known in England, as in some forms of ' Thrown Chair'; but these were not Windsors.

origin, it seems highly probable that, in its 'true' form, it was of English incidence. Even if this were not so, it must have very rapidly acquired a distinctive English impress—an impress as definite as is the American temper of the Colonial Windsor, which swiftly developed individual characteristics. Here, however, the situation is different, and, unless the English true-Windsor can be definitely pre-dated in substantial measure in other countries, we may continue to regard it as an English 'idea.'

So much for the mythos of our theme. Henceforth, and with a wary eye on Mr Gradgrind, we can devote ourselves as much as possible to FACTS.

CHAPTER II

The Method

I

First, a sprinkle of definitions. What do we mean by Windsor Chair; what, when the moment comes, by 'early'?

The latter term, at any rate, is relative; it excludes the proto-Windsors (actual or so-called) at which we have already glanced in passing. Primarily, it concerns the English product, leaving the American for separate discussion in Chapter IV. On this basis, an 'early' Windsor may be anything from the latter part of the seventeenth century, or more probably the early years of the eighteenth, to something after the middle of the eighteenth; and be it added that examples of this somewhat arbitrary period are not only difficult to acquire, but become progressively more difficult, as they near the *terminus a quo*. Such is a working rule-of-thumb, to which one pays just as much attention as is warranted by individual cases. Because various later types are available in quantity—though here again are rarities—it should never be supposed that any antique Windsor is either rare, or common. As ever, one must memorize the types—and use one's judgment.

On the matter of dating, let me sound a warning note. Quite a lot of antique furniture is datable within narrow limits, this particularly applying to pieces of modish and ultra-modish character. *Per contra*, the less fashionable or more countrified the item, the more difficult it is, in many cases, to feel confident of the justice of a narrow dating, when such furniture may not be *in* the mode but *following* it, perchance at some considerable distance. I have discussed this time-lag in another book,[7] so shall not dally with it here. The main point to be borne in mind is that furniture may be in the *style* of a given period without having been *made* in that same period, this especially applying to lesser-grade or country furniture—not in themselves derogatory terms. As the great majority of Windsors obviously belong to one or other of these rough-and-ready classifications, I decline to affect a datal precision which may be wide of the mark. Similarly, though such labels as 'Queen Anne', 'Chippendale', 'Sheraton', and 'Hepplewhite' are freely applied to Windsors, often with the slenderest justification, I find no good reason for using them more than is essential to a general understanding of current jargon. On the other hand, when a chair has been assigned, or is assignable, on good authority to a narrow dating, it seems advisable to record it, though elsewhere latitude is indulged, especially as regards the most popular and most repetitive types. The need for such latitudinarian treatment will be increasingly apparent as we trace the English Windsor through some two hundred and fifty years of history.

II

Next, the Windsor itself and its basic characteristics. It is an all-wood chair, or more rarely settee,[8] the back, mortised into the seat, being vertically railed and often, though far from always, furnished with one or more decorative banisters, or balusters, or splats. (As splat is the term most usually found in furniture-books, let us give it preference, albeit banister or, may be, baluster, would be the choice of an actual craftsman in Windsors.) In its earlier stages, the back has a plain or a shaped cresting. The seat throughout, is habitually cut from a single plank, saddle-shaped and 'dished', though variations occur, including an undished circular type; and in some late or modern Windsors cane or tension filling is introduced.* Back-rails, arm-supports (when present), and legs are plugged or tenoned into the seat. Legs and stretchers of various types will be noted as occasion demands, legs being either neatly turned or plain to roughness. As the eighteenth century progresses, the cabriole leg appears, and varieties of splat are numerous. The bow-back (to many the distinctive sign of a Windsor) is scarcely evident until well on in the latter part of the eighteenth century.

Many woods were used, among them oak, walnut, beech, ash, elm, yew, cherry, and various fruit-woods. The 'Common Windsor', says one account, 'was usually of beech with an ash bow and an elm seat', though, in fact, almost any available timber might be taken into use on occasion, especially for home-made chairs. Seats of elm were, however, frequent, and in Bucks the prevalence of beech, the 'Buckinghamshire weed', was a strong point in its favour for other parts. As *Murray's Hand-book* (*Berks, Bucks, and Oxfordshire*) says of the Wycombe trade in 1872, beech was 'employed for ordinary work, and walnut, birch, cherry, &c., for the better kinds'. Broadly speaking, there was (and had

---

* Windsors with upholstered seats (*i.e.* stuffed over the solid wood) were known in the past, though few antique examples have survived. For the evidence, see *Antiques*, July 1952, pp. 52-3; also *The Connoisseur*, June 1952, p. 47. All the examples illustrated at the references cited are assigned to the 1790's.

been) the craftsman's Windsor, and that dodged up by a local carpenter, as well as that made by the handy amateur minded to shape his own easement. There is, indeed, evidence to establish the existence of a moderately substantial output of quite locally-made furniture, as, for instance, 'in the hills' around High Wycombe, Princes Risborough, and nearby parts of the Chilterns: the more readily understandable in an area where the production of furniture has long been a staple industry. In such centres as Wycombe and the Risboroughs one still speaks of quite near-by places as 'in the hills' as though they were as geographically remote as the Rockies; and this local phrase, covering an indefinite number of villages, hamlets, and farmsteads, probably accounts also for a deal of local furniture before the centralization of the chair-making industry in Wycombe itself.

While Windsors have been acclaimed as the first bent-wood furniture, I do not wholly agree with the further description of them as the first mass-produced furniture. Apart from the detail that some earlier furniture (such, for instance, as the average seventeenth-century joined stool) could have been made by what were, relatively, mass-production methods, quite a number of Windsors show individual characteristics. All the same, the Windsor chair undoubtedly lent itself to mass-production, for the simple reason that it could be built up from pre-fabricated parts, and, whether or not it was originally regarded in such a light, it cannot have been long after the emergence of the true Windsor that the commercial possibilities of the method were seized upon by enterprising manufacturers.

Such was certainly the case long before the rise of chair-making as an industry in Wycombe in the early years of the nineteenth century, though it is reasonable to suppose that the craft was known there, if in an unorganized form, a good deal earlier than 1810, by which year what has been called the first factory of chairs there had already been established by Thomas Widgington. It was, however, more especially in the 1830's and '40's that the town became a focus of the craft. In noting this, one is far outstripping the chronology of Early Windsors, but the point must be made to dispel any lingering notion that Wycombe Windsors are necessarily of late appearance. If for Wycombe we read Wycombe area, it need not be doubted that Windsors were made thereabouts, whether by practised craftsmen or by moderately skilful amateurs, at least well back in the eighteenth century. Admitting that the presence of antique examples in or from that neighbourhood is not necessarily convincing, as old Windsors have been known to be brought into—perhaps, in some

Pl. 1. Early comb-back Windsor of elm, with late seventeenth-century features, but possibly of early eighteenth-century make.

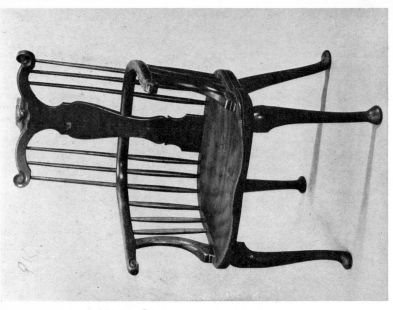

Pl. 2. Mutilated Windsor with unusual features. Note the finely curved arms, and the front legs with 'Spanish' feet.

Pl. 3. Windsor of good quality and possibly of Continental origin, in style about the second quarter of the

Pl. 4. Early Windsor of unusual form, its back showing the influence of a 'Queen Anne' type. Mid-eighteenth century.

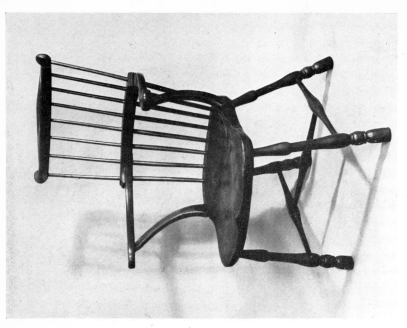

Pl. 6. Comb- or fan-back Windsor in certain respects resembling Oliver Goldsmith's Chair in the Victoria and Albert Museum, Middlesex.

Pl. 5. Fan-back Windsor of early type in ash with elmwood seat of rectangular formation. Eighteenth century.

Pl. 7. Comb-back Windsor, the arm-bow, sticks, and legs of ash, the seat of elm. Latter part of the eighteenth century (cf. Pl. 8).

Pl. 8. Comb-back Windsor of blackened wood, with primitive form of stretcher, and stick-back capped by a small cresting. Latter part of the eighteenth century.

Pls. 9 and 10. Fan-back Windsors with comb-cresting, representing a mid-eighteenth century type.

Pl. 11. American Writing Chair of maple and oak, the seat and writing-board of spruce. Assigned to c. 1775–1800.

Pl. 12. Elegant fan-back Windsor of the late eighteenth century, with cabriole legs and well-formed splat.

Pl. 13. Fine example of a comb-back Windsor Settee, *c.* 1760-70.

Pl. 14. American Settee, eighteenth century, 47 in. high, 39 in. wide.

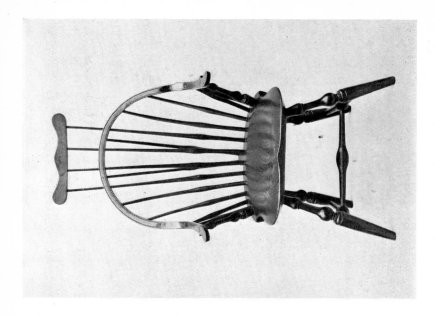

Pls. 15 and 16. American Windsors of a type combining bow- and comb-back; eighteenth century.

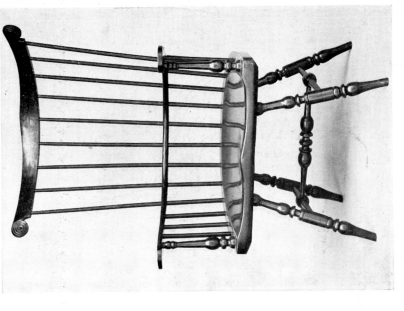

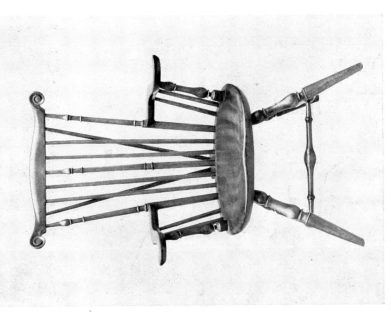

Pl. 17. American fan-back Windsor of pine, maple, oak, and ash; eighteenth century.

Pl. 18. Pennsylvania comb-back of spruce and oak. Assigned to c. 1750-75.

Pl. 19. Roomy comb-back Windsor with simple splat, and fore- and aft-cabrioles with solid brackets. Late eighteenth century.

Pl. 20. Plain stick-back type of Windsor 'bow', perhaps as early as the end of the eighteenth century.

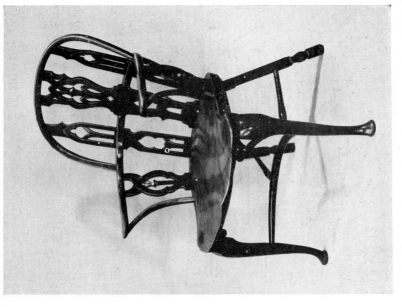

Pl. 22. Slightly later than Pl. 23, this 'Gothick' Windsor shows the same design adapted for use with a bow-back. Second half of the eighteenth century.

Pl. 21. 'Gothick' influence is seen in the upper part of the splat of this bow-back of the second half of the eighteenth century.

Pl. 23. The 'Gothick' Windsor at its most elaborate: a fine example of so-called 'Chippendale' taste of the second half of the eighteenth century.

Pl. 24. Bow-back Windsor, well formed in all its parts, of beech with elmwood seat. Late eighteenth century.

Pl. 25. Bow-back Windsor with semi-'Gothick' splat of so-called 'Chippendale' type, and cabriole fore-legs, the turned rear legs also having pad-feet. Late eighteenth century.

cases, brought back to—the area from London and elsewhere, there remains a quite sufficient quantity the local genesis of which cannot be reasonably doubted.

While on the matter of woods, be it noted that mahogany, if but rarely used for old Windsors, is not unknown in that connection. Though mahogany is, on average, less suitable than the 'homelier' woods for Windsors, it has been so used and not without success. In the Victoria and Albert Museum there is, for instance, a good stick-back chair which, if untypical, has distinct Windsor characteristics. Officially assigned to *circa* 1760-70, this plain if pleasing piece is stated to have belonged to the poet William Cowper (1731-1800).[9] Mahogany Windsors are extremely unusual, however, and have but little place in the collector's repertory.

The general preference for unfashionable woods sufficiently explains why so many Windsors, of widely varying ages, were either stained or painted, in the latter case usually black or green. Quite a number were left 'in the wood',* that is to say, in a self-coloured, unpolished state, either because the woods were seemly, or, much more often, so that 'house-proud cottagers could keep them clean by scouring with sand',[10] or some other cleanser. Sand was a good deal used for cleaning furniture left 'in the wood'. Have we not George Eliot's mention of 'sand-scoured tables so clean you longed to stroke them', in *Mr Gilfil's Love-Story* (originally published in 1857)? All the same, the number of chairs either painted or stained has always been considerable, and, in my opinion, a deal of damage has been done by stripping Windsors of their ancient paint or their pleasant warm-toned stain and varnish, under a misapprehension that such finishes were necessarily after-thoughts. Often enough, that comforting 'glow' which completes a Windsor's homely charm is due to its original surfacing with stain and varnish well worn by frequent polishing or use. However 'sticky' such chairs may have looked when new and raw, the effect, when thoroughly worked in, of their reddish humour, mellowed by time and happily contrasting with the natural tone of planes and angles exposed by normal friction, can be a relish to the eye.

One does not complain in instances when cleaning or reconditioning is rightly practised for the removal of accumulated filth or of many layers of clogging paint or modern varnish. What one has in mind is the stripping and scraping harshly practised by the well-intentioned in a desire to 'show

---

* In *A Short Dictionary of Oak Furniture* (1952; p. 503) Mr John Gloag records the trade term 'White Wycombe' for a Windsor left 'in the wood'.

C

the wood' of chairs never meant to be thus denuded. Unless done for an outstandingly valid reason, destruction of the original surface and patination of antique furniture is among the gravest kinds of antiquarian misdemeanour.

III

So far, we have merely glanced at the construction of Windsors. Let us now examine it in detail. Remembering that almost any available wood was used in making old examples, and that almost any combination of woods may be found in a given instance, there remain certain broad, guiding principles to which we can, in general, assent.

As has been seen, the seat was often fashioned in hard-wearing elm, whereas beech or ash supplied the legs, and ash or the pliant willow such curved members as the bow of the back or 'cow-horn' stretcher. Such is a reasonable approximation, subject to a wide range of variations; and it cannot be laid down that departures from the norm necessarily indicate repair or falsity, unless other evidence supports such a view. It must be borne in mind, however, that, as the 'utility' pieces they mostly were, Windsors underwent repairs, and replacements of this or that faulty member in the ordinary course of usage, and that some of these replacements may themselves be almost venerable. Though Windsors were the sort of furniture of which one easily grew fond—especially if one happened to be country-bred—they were not of much account in other ways; so why waste a good, usable chair just because it had lost a rail here, a leg there, or lacked the top of its back where too heavy a strain had been put upon it? One just mended the thing, if it was not too badly broken.

To such honest, if perhaps cloddish, botches are sometimes referable what have at first an air of being variations of type. Granted that true variations of type are numerous, the possibility of old repairs involving a change of form should be allowed for. Such may have happened in the case of certain chairs, apparently early examples of bow-back type, but showing on close inspection traces of comb-back construction. Either the back was broken and made good in a later style, or was brought up-to-date by elimination of the cresting to conform with other seating. When such repairs are obviously ancient, they are better left alone. Here, as ever, discrimination is advisable, but, saving grossly damaged or obviously desecrated pieces, my personal inclination is to leave an altered chair with its technical history as an open book for all to read who care to do so.

IV

As to manufacture, let us consider first the saddle-seat usually, though not invariably, a major characteristic of a Windsor. By 'saddle' is meant a seat of which the outline shows various forms of shaping more or less suggestive of a horse-saddle, the upper surface being 'dished' or hollowed to accommodate a sitter's thighs and buttocks. In many cases, though far from invariably, a V-shaped mount in front accommodates the fork, the whole seat being fashioned from a single plank or block of wood of a sufficient thickness to take the adze without risk of damage. On such chairs as were strengthened with back-braces—a couple of sticks diagonally inclined from seat to top, *behind* the ordinary sticks—a small supporting tongue or tail-piece, itself a part of the solid seat, was used as footing for these additional members. Windsors so equipped are often referred to as 'Brace-backs'.

It was quite usual for the various parts of a Windsor to be made by specialists: the main craftsmen employed being the Turner (or Bodger), the Benchman, and the Framer. The Turner was responsible for the legs, stretchers and sticks; the Benchman, 'for the cutting and rough finishing of the seat, bow, back splat, and any other sawn parts'; the Framer, for assembling and finishing.[11] Besides these, there were individual specialists, as Sawyers, Stainers, Polishers, and, of course, Seat-Makers (including the Bottomer and the Seat Cleaner Off*), and others to whom we shall nod in a later subsection. Splats, including the familiar 'wheel-back', were cut by a Bowsawyer. *Per contra*, there must always have been craftsmen, professional or amateur, who (like Goodchild, of whom more anon) were fully capable of achieving the whole process from start to finish.

In the Chilterns, a traditional form of the Turners' fraternity survives,

* Bottom here refers to the *seat* only of the chair, and not to the underframing generally, as some old quotations might seem to imply. Thus, in other types, we have leather-bottom, rush-bottom, cane-bottom, etc. As to Windsors, the man who adzed solid seats was known as a 'bottomer'; the seat was then cleaned off by a benchman; but if he did this solely he was known as a 'bottom cleaner off'. For this exact definition, which expands that of dictionaries, I am indebted to Mr F. H. Glenister. The term 'bottom-maker' is also found, but Mr Glenister does not think that it was in such common use as the terms given above. It was, however, specified in the Wycombe *Guide and Directory* of 1875.

such specialists still being known as Bodgers. In 1929, Sir Lawrence Weaver wrote that 'There were even lately bodgers who made the whole chair from the beginning. But that has practically ceased.'[12] Nowadays, a bodger is a maker of chair-legs first and foremost.

One or two bodgers, working more or less in the time-honoured way, even now survive, notably Mr Dean in the leafy Hampden Woods, 'in the hills' about midway between High Wycombe and the rapidly advancing outposts of the Aylesbury district. If sadly depleted in numbers, these bodgers carry on their ancient craft in a manner which, if now to some extent modernized by such details as the introduction of the power-driven lathe, is still in principle the same as ever. It was so simple as to make one marvel at the results achieved. Not only, in Weaver's words, did the bodgers 'in the main . . . devote themselves to making legs which are sent in their tens of thousands into High Wycombe', but 'the machine cannot beat handicraft at making and turning a leg.'[13]

The method (let us confine ourselves to the past) was for bodgers to 'buy at auction so many trees as they stand, set up their archaic huts nearby, and move on when the last billet has become a chair leg.'[14] Their small, thatched shacks were moved from site to site as the ground was cleared, the felled timber being hand-sawn into suitable lengths, split with an axe, and turned in the open or within the shanty's shelter 'with a pole-lathe so simple that it might have made the balusters of the Ark.'[15] The appropriateness of Weaver's pleasing simile can be appreciated by anyone who visits High Wycombe where a specimen pole-lathe with its simple but efficient 'treadle and cord drive' is (very properly) set up in the Museum, though unavoidably it now looks as dead as any Egyptian mummy awaiting an over-due resurrection.

May be it was on the last occasion when I visited 'Jack' Goodchild's workshop at Naphill that he pointed to a bundle of chair-legs which had come in from the bodgers. Though Goodchild was able to make an entire Windsor from start to finish on traditional lines, he was not above buying this or that part ready-made or partly finished, to save himself needless labour on the more humdrum items. Subject to correction, I seem to recall that the same was true of *some* of his splats, especially those of the common 'wheel' variety, though these, their perforations cut with a bow-saw, were also well within his capability. 'Better' chairs and particularly those of rare or elaborate design were, as far as I know, entirely his own work, and even in the lesser instances he doubtless improved and finished them with his own distinctive touch. If more the master-craftsman than the creative artist, 'Jack' Goodchild had an artist's love of his job, and as a maker of Windsors he stands second to none.

V

After being sawn from planks and roughly trimmed, chair-seats were adzed across the grain to form the requisite hollow. 'Jack' Goodchild himself gave me a demonstration of how this was done, the block being held in place by and between the craftsman's feet, which just gripped it at the sides. The block was then 'dished' with nicely calculated chopping strokes, the adze's cutting-edge being *towards* the maker. It was not the sort of thing one would care to try without knowing how. Next, the seat was worked on with the scraping tool called a 'travisher', held in both hands and worked against the grain. The seat had then to be bored for the reception of legs, sticks, and bow; and legs and bow had themselves to be bored as requisite, the latter to hold the sticks, the former to take the under-stretchers.

To make the bow (or hoop) of the back or other curved members, steaming or boiling was employed. Goodchild's method was to boil suitable lengths of yew in a metal cistern, this being a modernization of some earlier form of bath or steamer, as was the plate on which the by now flexible yew was quickly bent and pegged or tied in place until it had 'set'. In Goodchild's case, this plate was of iron, with holes pierced in it at regular intervals for the retaining pegs. As one authority has described the process as involving an 'iron block', it is worth noting that Goodchild himself told me that his own iron plate was an innovation, superseding a wooden block. The iron had the advantage of neither warping nor splitting, though his plate was not altogether what he could have wished, as the holes had not been quite correctly placed. Not that so skilled a craftsman was to be hampered by a little thing like that!

On this thick iron plate, 'powdered' (as the heralds say) with circular perforations, was mounted a wooden block or 'horseshoe mould' around which the steamed or, in Goodchild's case, the boiled yew was bent and pegged until dry and firm. This wooden block was detachable, and could be replaced by other moulds. The work of bending and fixing the bow was done swiftly, with sure hands, before the wood lost its pliancy. Such, then, was the bending of the bow. Modern mass production has replaced the block-and-peg technique by a machine which bends and holds the bows in place, a number at a time; but that is not a matter to concern the connoisseur.

VI

With the various parts of a Windsor to hand—and I am not attempting an exhaustive discussion of their manufacture—the next step was to assemble the chair. The seat, bow, back-rails, legs, and stretchers had all been bored when or as required. In many Windsors, the leg-sockets do not penetrate right through the seat, but in others the seats are holed for the fore-legs, so that the leg-tenon, wedged at its centre with a fox-tail wedge for tightness, is finished off flush with the upper surface.

I remember Goodchild showing me the first Windsor armchair he had made, many years before, and which he had kept for his own fancy. It looked pretty good, but Goodchild shook his head at it. He said he had not then had enough experience to tenon the leg *through* the seat. That was the way it *should* be done to ensure a nice firm fit. Be it added that it was, and is, by no means always employed, even on 'good' pieces; and that Goodchild himself countenanced the simpler 'blind' socket for items of lesser consequence.

With all its parts assembled, the chair underwent a general trimming by planing, filing, sand-papering, and the like, followed in many cases by finishing with stain and varnish, or may be paint. Goodchild's simple method was to plunge the chair in a bath of stain and next to polish it. For notes on staining as practised in the first half of the nineteenth century, the reader is referred to the *Appendix*.

It was in the final trimming, previous to staining, that such roughness as tenons projecting above seat-level were cut away—or so it was with Goodchild's chairs. In that great barn-like workshop of his at Naphill— a workshop crammed, piled, and hung with chairs and chair-parts in every stage of progress—were a few of his finest efforts: Windsors of superb and elaborate quality—particularly one Gothick Windsor which (he said) he could not bring himself to finish and deliver—because he thought so highly of it!

Besides a considerable stock of unassembled parts, there were, too, chairs of other patterns, finished or in progress at the time of Goodchild's death. Of one excellent chair, with 'Chippendale' splat and cabriole front legs, since acquired for High Wycombe Museum, Mr L. John Mayes has told me that Goodchild had rejected it for no more reason than a tiny flaw in the upper part of the bow. On account of that almost invisible hair-line split, Goodchild would neither sell that lovely chair nor give it away! Therein we have the measure of the fastidious taste apparent in every Windsor for which 'Jack' Goodchild was himself responsible.

VII

Not infrequently, though far from always, Windsors were 'signed' by the benchman concerned, usually by an impressed mark on the back edge of the seat, consisting of initials sometimes followed by a pattern-number. In certain cases, initials are identifiable by reference to the records of chair-making concerns, or to old directories. Modern marks also exist. Broadly speaking, old marks fall into one of two classes: 'blind' stamps neatly designed in a manner more or less comparable with the 'touches' of silversmiths or pewterers, and initials rather roughly stamped with individual punches, pattern-numbers being added in the same way. For example, an antique 'Prince of Wales' feathers' chair, now belonging to Mrs Michael Maynard, is neatly impressed on its tail-piece with a script ES in a rectangular compartment, and the Smoker's Bow in Pl. 46 with DH in a kidney-shaped compartment. These belong to the former class of marking; of the latter, made with separate punches, it will suffice to mention Mrs Michael Maynard's two old wheel-splat Windsors bearing a punched TA on the tail-piece; whereas the Berger Bow in Pl. 47 is punched with initials readable as D.G. 163, quite probably in allusion to a Wycombe maker, Daniel Glenister. Any curious student of Windsors will be able to add to the list of such marks, some of which may well allude to makers, though others may have a different significance, such as ownership—a not impossible contingency in the case of chairs ordered in bulk for public or semi-public usage, as a precaution against theft or other unauthorized removal.

The possibility of Windsors being signed in other ways cannot be ignored; Mr Desmond Butler has told me of a Smoker's Bow both named and dated in the 1880's, and it may be that earlier instances, if rare, exist. For the most part, however, Windsors are anonymous, and even some of the most skilled makers seem never to have adopted the practice of marking. So far as I know, 'Jack' Goodchild never 'signed' his work, though I asked him more than once to make a Windsor specially for me, with his name on one side of the seat and with mine on the other. He said with all courtesy that he would consider it—it was evidently the sort of commission that called for contemplation—but that unique Goodchild Windsor will never reach me now. Temperamentally, Goodchild was typical of the lone craftsman and in talking to him one noticed his dislike of submitting his talent to the restraints of organized corporations; whereas in Thomas Widgington, of High Wycombe, who flourished a century or more earlier, one discerns a prototype of 'big business', though his start was modest enough.

I had hoped that precise records of Widgington might have survived in his family's possession, but Alderman R. A. Janes, of High Wycombe, who has courteously helped my inquiry, and who was himself apprenticed to 'best chairmaking' in 1885, has informed me that such is not the case. As a Wycombe notable, Widgington has attained an almost mythical stature, though some facts about him are recoverable.

Something of this mythical aura surrounds Sir Lawrence Weaver's statement that 'Samuel Treacher and Thomas Widgington seem to have been the Chippendales of the Windsor Chair [in Wycombe] in the last quarter of the eighteenth century, for they are commemorated in stained glass in the Mayor's Parlour at the Town Hall.'[16] If to some extent true, Weaver's words are a little misleading. Alderman Janes has informed me that Samuel Treacher, who farmed Hill Farm on the top of Marlow Hill, started his chair-making about 1805 as a winter occupation for his hands, and that Widgington, whose own chairmaking business was begun a few years later, 'came to Wycombe' to teach Treacher's men how to assemble chairs from the parts supplied by the bodgers. It is, however, certain that by 1837 Treacher was a fairly substantial property-owner in Wycombe Foreigns, where were his own house and Chair Manufactory. At this time other Treachers (among them Samuel, Junior) were tenant-farming in the Wycombe area: and Widgington owned three houses in Temple Place, Wycombe Foreigns. (*A Valuation of the Houses . . . in the Parish of Chepping Wycombe, Bucks.* [1837] MS., High Wycombe Public Library.)

Widgington himself was buried in the west corner of that piece of the graveyard of High Wycombe Parish Church which was separated from the main burial ground when Castle Street was cut through it. His headstone survives, giving his date of death as 18 January, 1846, and his age as 74. He would thus have been born about 1772, though whence he 'came to Wycombe', if indeed he did so, is problematical. It so happens that a 'Thomas, son of William and Elizabeth Wigington' (*sic*), was baptized at High Wycombe Parish Church, 22 September 1771; and numerous entries in the registers of Great Marlow (a few miles away) show that persons named Wiginton, Wigington, and kindred spellings, were to be found in the latter parish over an extensive period.[17] I have no proof that any of these was related to our chairmaker, or that he was identical with the Thomas Wigington who was baptized at Wycombe in 1771; but if, in fact, he was so, it might perhaps be argued that it was not Thomas Widgington, but his father, who 'came to' Wycombe; unless, perchance, Thomas himself had been away from Wycombe and merely returned to it.

All this is pure hypothesis, subject to the discovery of more reliable evidence; but that our Thomas Widgington (already an experienced chairmaker) was in Wycombe about 1805, and instructing Treacher's 'hands', is not improbable. That Widgington *was* settled in Wycombe not much later than this is shown by another headstone, next to his (and much better preserved) in High Wycombe churchyard. This commemorates two of his children: Thomas, son of Thomas and Sarah Widgington, died 21 April, 1808, age 2 years and 9 months, and a daughter Sarah, died 2 February, 1814, aged 10 years and 8 months. Alderman Janes, who put me on the track of these gravestones, has gathered for me a tradition that young Thomas (1808) 'was burned to death, according to family recollections'. I have failed to trace this tragedy in such periodicals of the time as I have consulted. Widgington himself died intestate, admon. of his estate being granted to his eldest (surviving) son Samuel Widgington, 16 June, 1846 (Arch. Bucks.). In it, deceased was described as Thomas Widgington of Chepping Wycombe, Chair Manufacturer, and the estate was sworn at the nominal sum of 'under £100'.

Samuel Treacher's origin is also obscure, but I am advised that a Samuel, son of William and Hannah Treacher, was baptized at High Wycombe Parish Church, 26 November, 1769. He was doubtless our man. Samuel Treacher and Martha Allen were married, by licence, at Wycombe, 21 May, 1807[18]; and our Samuel was buried there 27 September, 1845— the day being seemingly at variance with that carved on his headstone in the churchyard, which appears to indicate that he died 28 September, 1845, in his 76th year. The inscriptions on this and other Treacher memorials near the S.E. angle of the main churchyard are much weathered. There are no fewer than five Treacher headstones in a line there, with yet one more, flanking and somewhat in advance of them, in the manner of a grim and crumbling N.C.O. Samuel's pedimental stone, in the midst of this silent rank, records his mother Anna (*sic*), first wife of William Treacher. Both Samuel and William (the latter on a separate stone) are 'of this parish', and William's widow seems to have been named Hannah. The detail that William and Samuel Treacher, and, on his own stone, Thomas Widgington, are all described as 'Mr' suggests that they were or had become persons of superior standing; and in his will (dated 21 January, 1845, proved 6 February, 1846, P.P.C.) Treacher went a stage further, describing himself as 'of the parish of Chepping Wycombe . . . Gentleman'. His son and exor. William Allen Treacher, is therein cited as farmer. Presumably Samuel Treacher had by then retired from active business, but that he had a chair-factory in Wycombe by at any rate the 1830's is demonstrable.[16]

Interesting as it would be to identify Treacher's chairs, I know of no means of so doing. Indeed, Alderman Janes has given me as his opinion that he doubts 'if any have survived after being knocked up in a barn by semi-skilled farm labourers'. A delightful comment, but one never knows! Whether or not Treacher's local fame has become somewhat over-shadowed is a point I have been unable to decide.

Neither Treacher nor Widgington can have had any idea that their names would come to be commemorated in stained glass: an apotheosis as unusual for chairmakers as it is appropriate to Wycombe, though, in noting it, we must bear in mind that 'Wycombe Chairs' were not, and are not, necessarily of Windsor type. Such forms as the traditional 'cottage' ladder-back with rush seats were made there, as were, in Victorian times, such later developments as the 'balloon-back', the 'camel-back', the 'Rise and Drop', the 'Double C', and numerous other designs, some of which are indicated in the present writer's *Victorian Furniture* (Phoenix House Ltd). For all that, Windsors were made in large numbers in and around High Wycombe, and seem to have formed a sizable part of manu-facturers' output there.

Such was certainly the case when the Wycombe chair industry was fairly under way. To Thomas Widgington, however, is assigned the credit of having established the first actual chair-making factory in High Wycombe. This was not later than 1810, the premises being a tiny, two-storey building in St Mary's Street. Here, with a few other craftsmen, Widgington is stated to have set up the first Wycombe chair-making business to be run on something approaching factory methods, as apart from the efforts of solitary or relatively unorganized craftsmen, whether in Wycombe itself, the surrounding neighbourhood, or 'in the hills'. Some of Widgington's men eventually left to set up their own businesses, says Alderman Janes; and small though were the beginnings of Widging-ton's enterprise, it was fated to stimulate the rise of the industry in

Wycombe. This remained commercially unremarkable until the 1830's or early 1840's, but by the '60's had grown so greatly that 'Wycombe Chairs' were being made in enormous quantities for export far and wide.

At that time, it was claimed (as recorded by Sheahan) that Wycombe chairs, including of course other types as well as Windsors, were being made at the rate of one a minute for each working day of the year, but during 1874 this average was increased to more than seven chairs per minute. Thus *A Local Guide and Directory for the Town of High Wycombe* (preface dated July 1875), which adds that the total did not include the chairs made 'in West Wycombe, Downley, Lane End, Stokenchurch, etc., which outlying villages probably turn out as many as were made in the town itself some twenty years ago'.

Among the many firms producing Windsors in High Wycombe there is present cause to note that, founded in 1839, of Daniel Glenister, who was in business under the name of Glenister & Son until 20 March, 1865, when he retired in favour of his son Thomas Glenister and his son-in-law Charles Gibbons. I am much indebted to Mr F. H. Glenister and to Mr W. R. Butler of Messrs Thomas Glenister Ltd for this information and for telling me that the Glenister & Gibbons partnership was dissolved in 1879, the business now being perpetuated under the name of the said Thomas Glenister, who died in 1919. 'The business carried on by Charles Gibbons became extinct about thirty years ago.' The years are important as a chair specifically made by Glenister & Gibbons in concert can thus be narrowly dated, though there is no reason to doubt that in certain cases they continued models already existent. For example, the Berger Bow seen in Pl. 47 is stamped DG 163 on the back-edge of the seat. The G is indistinct, but it seems probable that this chair was framed by Daniel Glenister *circa* 1850-65, though the model is exactly rendered in a Glenister & Gibbons' catalogue (therein pl. 31, no. 139) of *circa* 1865-79, of which more anon. The pattern (or model) number does not agree, but this may have been changed at some time. Unfortunately, details of transactions by Daniel Glenister himself are not known to have survived.

The popularity of Windsors in the middle and second half of the nineteenth century is well shown by certain old pattern-books now in High Wycombe Public Library. One of the most interesting is an oblong volume, suitable for a capacious pocket, containing numerous careful water-colour drawings, the pages being interleaved with a thin and pinkish blotting-paper. Like many other old pattern-books, this has suffered by frequent usage and is now incomplete, but a modern, type-written title-page describes it as *Chair Designs by Walter Skull 1849*.[19]

The firm of Walter Skull & Co. Ltd still exists in Wycombe, where the name of Skull is a household word. A similar book of drawings, in water-colour with additions in pencil, belongs to Messrs Thomas Glenister Ltd. The technique of the water-colour is close to that of the Skull book, but Mr F. H. Glenister informs me that he has always understood that the drawings in his volume were done by his grandfather, Thomas Glenister, whose name appears in it. Whether this implies that the Glenister drawings were made after 1879, or whether (as seems to me possible) the name was stamped in an already existent book after the dissolution of the Glenister and Gibbons partnership, I am unable to decide.

To the 1860's or '70's can be ascribed two other pattern-books or trade-catalogues, mutilated copies of which are preserved in High Wycombe Public Library, both carrying a considerable number of lithographed plates on a larger scale than Skull's, but, like it, including a variety of Windsors as well as other chairs. These lithographed catalogues are B.N: *Antique and Plain and Ornamental Chairs* (Alfred Reeves & Co., Printers, 18 Finsbury Street, Chiswell Street, London); [20] and G. & G.: *Patterns of Cane, Windsor, Fancy & Other Chairs*,[21] the latter's binding being impressed (beneath the Royal Arms of Queen Victoria) with the full name of the previously mentioned firm of Glenister and Gibbons, Oxford Street, High Wycombe. B.N. presumably stands for Benjamin North, of West Wycombe, whose chair-making business was started in 1852, and was well established and active by 1862 when J. J. Sheahan described it in his *History and Topography of Buckinghamshire*. The approximate date of the G. & G. catalogue is fixed by the detail that the partnership of Glenister & Gibbons was from 1865-1879, as previously mentioned. All three catalogues, Skull's, B.N.'s, G. & G.'s, testify to the popularity of Windsors, G. & G. illustrating no fewer than fifty-six varieties as against some thirty-two of Skull's. It is, too, interesting to note the per-sistence of purely 'Georgian' types or details, side-by-side with more recent, if not necessarily more admirable, developments. On one of B.N.'s pages, one notes a regrettable hybrid in which a late Windsor frame is provided with a cane-back. As making the worst of both worlds, it has but little to commend it. Fortunately, the maintenance of the Windsor tradition in chair-making has been perpetuated on sounder lines than this.

Anyone desirous of making a minute inquiry into the actual names of manufacturers and craftsmen in the 1870's will find much to his purpose in *A Local Guide and Directory for the Town of High Wycombe*, the preface of which is dated July 1875. The number of benchmen, seat-makers, turners, back-makers, bottom-makers (that term being preferred to the more colloquial if much used 'bottomers'), chair-stainers, polishers, Windsor framers, and others listed therein is impressive, and it is noteworthy how such craftsmen tended to congregate in certain quarters of the town. Railway Place was teeming with them; so was Saffron Platt, and so—but to our theme.

At no time since has the production of Windsors ceased in High Wycombe, and to-day, when that town is among the most important centres of the furniture industry, it is pleasant to note that, among the numerous and sometimes outstanding chairmaking firms in business there, old Thomas Widgington's tiny two-storey building in St Mary's Street, survives, incorporated in the well-known house of Messrs Nicholls & Janes Ltd, of which a great-great-grandson of his (Mr R. W. Boreham) is a director. That Windsors are still regarded locally with an affectionate pride is evident to those who, like the present writer, have lived in the district. At Princes Risborough, for instance, many cottages and modest dwellings, to say nothing of inns and other places of public resort, are still equipped as a matter of course with Windsor Chairs of this or that variety—some new, or nearly so, others of a respectable elderliness. And when in 1950 the Wycombe Wanderers Football Club made a gift to the Bungay Town F.C., the presentation took the sensible and enlightened form, not of some grandiose cup or trophy, but of a good, sound, ordinary bow-back, wheel-splat, Windsor of traditional design.[22] Would that it were always thus on such occasions! That there was good precedent for this gesture is evident in other directions, as when the Chair Manufacturers of High Wycombe presented a somewhat heavily built and double-stretchered Smoker's Bow to Lieut.-Colonel Gerard Smith, as the last M.P. for the borough of Chepping Wycombe, 1883-85.

So much for an aspect of our theme which deserves a passing tribute.

Before going on to other matters, let us pay a final visit to 'Jack' Goodchild in his picturesquely cluttered workshop at Naphill, 'in the hills', betwixt Wycombe and the Risboroughs.

VIII

News travels fast in country places. Bush telegraph had told me that 'Jack' Goodchild was out of health before the news of his death was published in the *Bucks Free Press* for 8 December, 1950. Such was his local fame that he was then given an obituary of some length, as well as an editorial in a later issue of the same newspaper. Since then, one of his chairs and a

representative collection of his tools and other contents of his workshop
have very properly been acquired for High Wycombe Museum; for,
though 'Jack' Goodchild created no new types of Windsor, his place as a
maker of traditional Windsors is second to none and better than most of
any period. He once told me that his ambition was to have made every
known type of Windsor, a tall enough order when one contemplates
a possible total running into three figures, though when I put it to him
that it would be interesting to invent a new kind, it was easy to tell that
the suggestion evoked no responsive interest. That was in the last years
of his life, and if he had not achieved his ideal of making every existing
type, he must have realized an appreciable part of it.

But if 'Jack' Goodchild was not in grain a creator, he was very far
from being a slavish imitator, though he could and, on occasion, did
repair antique Windsors as a sideline. It was not merely that his own
Windsors were superlatively made, reproducing retrospective designs
with a remarkable fidelity, but that his sense of proportion and his nice
judgment of planes and angles imparted a distinction to his work fully
meriting the epithet 'Goodchild Windsors'. I confess I have been troubled
by the thought that some of the best of his chairs, such as his elaborate
'Gothick' Windsors, might run some risk of being artificially aged and
passed as eighteenth-century examples were they to fall into unscrupulous
hands; but Goodchild himself had no thought of such eventualities. His
work, to use a convenient phrase, is 'signed all over', and he himself was
unmistakably the honest master-craftsman who loved his work for what
(as he told me) he could learn from it.

In a modest way, befitting the modest man he was, Goodchild's reputa-
tion is already more than local. He and his workshop are the subject of
a characteristic etching by Stanley Anderson, R.A. He had figured in
films and radio-references, and still photographs of him at work are
numerous (Pl. 54). He figures in more books and articles than I shall
attempt to list. Some of these are informative, though of Goodchild
as a personality I know of no livelier account than Adrian Bury's article
on *Mr Goodchild's Immortal Chairs* in *Everybody's* for 2 October, 1948.
As I accompanied Adrian when he visited Goodchild to gather material
for this article, I can testify to the soundness of its 'atmosphere'.

A native of Naphill, where he was born on 25 February, 1885,[23] 'Jack'
Goodchild's actual fore-names were Harold Edward, a point worth
noting if a future generation of commentators is to avoid an almost
pardonable duplication of identity. To all who knew him, Harold Edward
Goodchild was always 'Jack'. His father (William Goodchild) and grand-

father had both been makers of Windsor chair-seats, whence 'Jack's' skill with the adze in this particular.

He himself was a smallish, trim-built figure of a man, quick in movement, with the alert gaze and the projecting, well-formed, slightly 'inquiring' nose not infrequently characteristic of good craftsmen. He sported a small moustache, twisted to points, his unthinning hair being neatly parted on his left side, with the fore-lock swept back from his forehead. Though conscious of his worth, he was unassertive. You might have taken Goodchild for an ex-serviceman with subsequent service as a special constable, and your guess would have been well founded.

'Besides his work', ran his obituary in the *Bucks Free Press* of 12 December, 1950, 'Mr Goodchild had served as a special constable in the Bucks Constabulary since 1926, and he was a chorister at Hughenden Parish Church. During the first world war he served with the Oxford and Bucks Light Infantry in Mesopotamia'. He died at Naphill on 1 December, 1950, aged 65, and lies buried at Hughenden Parish Church, in the same graveyard as a more conspicuous artist in other media, Benjamin Disraeli, Earl of Beaconsfield.

CHAPTER III

English Windsors

I

FOR the purpose of this book, and on the basis as laid down at the start of the previous Chapter, 'Early Windsors' is held to cover, not the actual or so-called prototypes, but indisputable Windsors dating from the first half of the eighteenth century, with an overlap of possibly some ten or more years either way. Be it emphasized that this is rough approximation, liable to be modified by the emergence of hitherto unrecorded evidence. Even so—and this again must be repeated—many a Windsor is likely to remain difficult to date within narrow limits, owing to the tenacity of traditional elements. Once absorbed into the Windsor repertory and having become popular, a given design might be repeated changelessly, or nearly so, for a lengthy period—as witness such surviving types as the 'wheel-splat', which has been made for anything up to 150 years.

Thus, a chair in the general style of, say, 1800 might easily have been fashioned fifty or more years later, and may even be of recent date. In such instances, it often happens that one can do little more than separate the obviously older from the patently later items. *Per contra*, 'period' pieces can not infrequently be detected, though it is wise to bear in mind that vagaries of wear and tear, of much polishing on the one hand or contemptuous mishandling on the other, may have the effect of increasing an appearance of antiquity.

Such possibilities must be allowed for, in addition to considerations of style and construction, before one reaches a decision as to the age of problematical items. Moreover, faking, as apart from honest if misguided smashery, cannot be entirely ruled out, though, in general, it is only the rarest types of Windsor that are likely to interest the purveyor of falsities.

Which being said, let us come to grips with our Early Windsors.

II

As briefly outlined in Chapter I, attempts have been made to trace the Windsor form from prototypes. These mainly, though not entirely, consist of low-back chairs, scarcely higher than the waist or base of the shoulder-blades of a seated occupant. If one takes, say, Pl. 2 in this book, or Pl. 1, in the latter case ignoring everything above the arm-bow (*i.e.* the line of the arms and mid-retaining band), one has a fairly good idea of what is meant. By extension upwards, such a piece assumes a Windsor shape as known to everyone.

A difficulty here is that the true Windsor (so to call it) emerges fully fledged, and that, in the case of a tall chair backed with slender sticks, a strengthening member at more or less the midway point is, in many instances, if not a structural necessity, at least desirable. Nevertheless, it is interesting to consider the case of such low-built true Windsors as the Smoker's Bow (Pl. 46), though most surviving English examples of this are of late or even recent date. That this popular chair is a modest edition of the typical Georgian Elbow- or Corner-Chair must not blind us to the fact that its ancestry also takes in the low-back Windsor of which eighteenth-century examples are, perhaps, more frequently found in American collections. The development of the tall-back Windsor from a low-back type is at least a possibility, though the process may not have followed any definite system of progression. Indeed, the most superficial examination of certain late tall-back Windsors, including some of the (so-called) Yorkshire or Lancashire type, shows clearly enough that such a process was adopted, or reverted to, in the nineteenth century, such chairs being no more than ordinary Smoker's Bows with a hoop, sticks, and splat superimposed on the back (Pls. 39 and 40). The bows are not prolonged to seat level.

To those unversed in Windsors, the name probably suggests a wooden-seated, bow-backed chair, and that alone. In fact, there are a number of other basic types, and the bow-back is not present on true Early Windsors, of which the sticks are topped by a plain or ornamental cresting. In collectors' parlance, such chairs are known as 'comb-back' (Pls. 1, 3, 7, etc.), or, when the back is noticeably splayed, as 'fan-back' (Pls. 5, 9, 10, etc.), the comb-type being probably the earlier of the two in so far as Windsors are concerned, though in due course they were made contemporaneously. There is nothing recondite in these descriptive terms, and the distinction between them is artificial. One has only to glance at a hair-comb, or, better, the business end of a wooden hay-rake to see why comb-backs are so-called. As for the 'fan', the back is literally fanned out, V-wise; or if you will, is vaguely suggestive of a part-furled fan.

One of the earliest true Windsors is that in Pl. 1, a stick-back chair of elm, its elaborately shaped and partly perforated cresting bearing a crown of a kind relating it to those other chairs carved with crowns or

D

'boyes and crowns'—two *putti* supporting a crown—which used to be
classed as 'Restoration Furniture'—Restoration in this case meaning the
return of King Charles II from exile in Holland. It has, however, been
established that many of these so-called 'Restoration Chairs' date from no
earlier than the last three decades of the seventeenth century, and that
if some were made not at the virtual beginning, but towards the close,
of the Merry Monarch's reign, others are demonstrably later than his
death.[24] The chair in question is further equipped with slender 'barley-
sugar' rails in the position of a splat, and retains its original front-rail
and stretcher also of 'barley-sugar' type. The capacious seat is dished, and
the arm-supports are bowed to leave an opening between them and the
nearest upright. 'The spiral turning, and the crown . . . indicate a date
about 1685', says Macquoid and Edwards' *Dictionary*, but the known
tendency of the makers of Windsors to lag well behind the vogue inclines
one to Mr Symonds' opinion that there is no reason to suppose that such
chairs 'would be of an earlier date than 1720'.[25] Junction of the seventeenth
and eighteenth centuries might be a generous estimate of the period of
this particular item. Be it noted that not every Windsor ensigned with a
crown is necessarily of early date, as bow-backs with a *splat* carved and
pierced with a crown were made in the earlier part of the nineteenth
century, but these are of different character.

It will be noticed that whereas some stick-back chairs rely on the sticks
alone to fill the back, others are further strengthened with a splat or
banister. At a considerably later stage than that now under discussion,
as many as three splats are sometimes found in one chair back, though one
is the normal allowance. The omission of any splat does not indicate
per se an early piece, as plain stick-backs were made consistently throughout the whole of the true Windsor's history, surviving the change from
comb- to bow-back, and through to modern times. Crestings, whether
straight or slightly curved, plain or shaped on their upper edge, also
possessed a 'survival value', for, though largely ousted from favour by
the introduction of the bow, they tended (mainly in their less ornamental
forms) to recrudesce in principle if not necessarily in general effect. Of
this more anon, but as the primary purpose of a cresting is to hold the
back together, there is nothing untoward in its recurrence, so far as any
generalization can be indulged. Of the two main types of cresting, plain
and shaped, the latter seems to have been the earlier on true Windsors,
but shaping was continued for a while after the plain cresting had vir-
tually swept the board.

If, so far as Early Windsors are concerned, comb-back chairs are normal, one should be prepared for other forms of construction, as is shown by the very unusual Windsor in Pl. 4. However tempting it may be to detect in this rare item a transitional stage between the comb-back and the bow-, its true affinity is with a type of so-called 'Queen Anne' chair which reached its full development of humps and curves between about 1725-45. It is, no doubt, a rustic attempt to adapt a townish idiom to the Windsor pattern, though it seems scarcely likely such could have been a regular design, produced in quantity. This somewhat eccentric Windsor has been assigned to *circa* 1740, a date with which it is difficult to quarrel, though the greater latitude allowed by so convenient a term as 'mid-eighteenth century' may be preferred by some, in view of the tendency to rural time-lag in design. Though now shortened, the front-legs are a rustic attempt to emulate the cabriole, and the side-stretchers with a 'swell' towards the front are related at some removes to the side-stretchers, hipped at the front end, on the earlier Windsor in Pl. 1.

One of the key-pieces in normal Windsor design of the earlier sort is the now famous 'Goldsmith Chair' in the Victoria and Albert Museum (538-1872), of which a near-relation, though omitting the splayed back-brace, is seen in Pl. 6. As chairs more or less of this type are now freely spoken of as 'Goldsmith Chairs', it should be made clear that the sole basis for the title is that the example referred to at South Kensington is known to have belonged to Oliver Goldsmith. He bequeathed it, on his death in 1774, to his friend William Hawes, M.D., founder of the Royal Humane Society: and it was the widow of Sir Benjamin Hawes (1797-1862) who gave it to the Museum in 1872.[26] Its pedigree, therefore, is as well supported as can be expected, and it is no fault of the V. & A. authorities that their exhibition of this interesting piece has given rise to the labelling as 'Goldsmith' of a rabble of chairs which never had any association with the great Irish writer. With the solitary exception of the South Kensington chair, 'Goldsmith', as a descriptive label, has as much force as that of 'Chippendale Windsor'.

The South Kensington chair is officially assigned to the mid-eighteenth century. That, more or less, may be accepted as the approximate period of other examples nearly resembling it, though persistence of type may well bring some others to well on in the second half of the eighteenth century. Moreover, a revival of the form towards the end of the Victorian period must also be allowed for. As a rule, these and other modern examples are easily detectable.

It may be noted that not a few of these recent (usually fan-back) chairs have an entirely circular seat, in which they follow some antique examples.

One such, in Aylesbury Museum, has been either made or converted as a Close-Chair, though the hole has since been plugged. This chair is painted green, whereas black, or nearly so, is the present colour of Goldsmith's chair at South Kensington, though it has in the past been described as green, and is so specified in a pencil sketch by that eminent antiquary Edward Blore, F.R.S., F.S.A. (1787-1879) now in the Library of the Royal Institute of British Architects.* In both this chair and the one at Aylesbury the seat is circular, dished, and furnished with a fork-support. Other examples exist, though many so-called 'Goldsmiths' have seats of ordinary saddle-type, perhaps because, in an essentially broad-beamed century, this was on the whole the more utilitarian form; but before unhesitatingly assigning chairs of 'Goldsmith' type to the mid-eighteenth century, it is wise to study them closely. Undished circular seats also occur. Not all such chairs are as early as the veritable Oliver Goldsmith's Chair at South Kensington. Some, indeed, are wholly modern.

Among the marks of an Early Windsor (so far as anything is assured when traditional methods are in question) is the fashion of the legs. These may be roughly trimmed, spoke-shaved, or neatly turned, for all three persisted side-by-side. The plain baluster-turning on the early Windsor in Pl. 1 explains itself, and another characteristic type, slender and with a hipped member, is seen in Pls. 6 and 7. This, if by no means an infallible indication of earliness, is a detail worth watching when taken in conjunction with other characteristics. Stretchers, too, are of a simple kind, many being braced by a cross-piece at the central point. As representing a primitive form of this construction, Pl. 8 is interesting. It perpetuates an ancient method of locking the cross-bar *through* the side-stretchers, whereas, in general practice, the custom was, and is, to bore the latter for the reception of the cross-bar, which fitted tightly into, without piercing, them. But though this particular chair perpetuates traditional methods, it is probably nothing like as early as its simplicity suggests. The bowing of the sticks to fit into an unusually small cresting suggests to me a local attempt to emulate the bow-back without actually employing a retaining hoop; and, as the chair is believed to have come from Wales, where ancient methods lingered, it seems unsafe to assign it to anything earlier than the latter part of the eighteenth century. A small cresting with straight sticks is, however, found in other and sometimes earlier examples in both England and America. This feature is prominent in Pl. 7, which in its owners' view is 'probably Dutch', though no evidence of its source is

* Press-mark H4/51; Sketch-book in which the date 1876 occurs. I am indebted to my friend Mr Cyril G. E. Bunt for drawing my attention to this item.

available. It is worth noting that a New Jersey Windsor illustrated in Wallace Nutting's *Furniture Treasury* (New York: Macmillan Co., 1948, Fig. 2594), also shows sticks slightly bowed to fit into a small-sized comb. That this was intentional and not, as Nutting assumed, due to the comb not being long enough is indicated by the examples noted above.

To say that the under-framing of side-stretchers and cross-bar was superseded by the curved member called 'cow-horn' stretcher (or, less happily 'crinoline-stretcher'), as seen in Pls. 21, 22, 23, is incorrect. If the 'cow-horn' (so called from its shape) became prominent about the middle of the eighteenth century, continuing in favour for several decades, the older, simpler method was anything but discarded and, indeed, out-lasted its rival. Occasionally Windsors are found with two cow-horn stretchers, placed back to back, but the eventual abandonment of the device (in whatever form) is assignable to the greater ease of turning straight lengths of wood, thus reducing the steaming or boiling necessary for producing large numbers of minor bows, including, at an appropriate period, arm-supports. But as these considerations take us well on into the second half of the eighteenth century (and later), it is as well to pause and take stock.

III

When the bow-back, as such, was first adopted for Windsors is by no means clear, though writers in both England and America have assigned its introduction to as far back as about the middle of the eighteenth century. On the other hand, surviving English examples of early character seldom suggest anything previous to the second half or, more frequently, the last quarter of that epoch. One superficially early example of English origin known to me, in which cabriole legs and a stick-back are combined with a simple bow imposed *above* the arm-bow, suggested, on close examination, that the bow-top was an afterthought, and that the chair had originally been a comb-back which may have sustained damage and been rather roughly repaired in the newer fashion at a later date. It is, however, evident that English bow-backs were in being by the 1790's as two plain stick-backs of that formation figure in a picture by Samuel de Wilde of *Mr R. Palmer as Tag in the Spoil'd Child* exhibited at the Royal Academy in 1797, and now belonging to the Garrick Club, from which it was lent for 'The First Hundred Years of the Royal Academy' at Burlington House, 1951-52 (No. 125). These chairs, which are depicted in an outdoor setting, have turned legs of a plainer type than that in vogue not much later, and both are painted a lively green.

As to that other innovation (so far as Windsors are concerned) the cabriole leg, it should be noted that this never ousted the turned leg, which persisted alongside and survived it. The Cabriole was for a good while popular on Windsors, more especially for higher-grade chairs, though even so rustic an affair as Pl. 4 shows a vague attempt to realize the form. The cabriole seems to have entered the Windsor repertory relatively late; long after it was a well-established adjunct of other classes of furniture. Old Windsor Chairs and, rarer, Settees exhibiting this feature usually belong to the second half of the eighteenth century; but seldom are they at all likely to ante-date the mid-century. Indeed, Windsors with more than a smack of 'Queen Anne' about them have been assigned on good authority to *circa* 1760-70, or even later (*e.g.* Pl. 13). For the most part, cabrioles were used as fore-legs only, the rear legs being turned. Some Windsors, however, have cabrioles at both front and back, though this is relatively rare. Interesting and desirable as good 'cabriole Windsors' are, one can but agree with Mrs Therle Hughes's comment that 'few designers found any satisfactory line for the union of curving leg and block seat.'[27] Superior antique examples exist in which the difficulty has been overcome (*e.g.* Pls. 22, 27), but in many cases the cabrioles look 'stuck on', and fail to form an integral part of the design. In some cases this is due to the applied brackets having fallen off, but in others it was seemingly enough to give a chair its cabriole legs and leave it at that; and this defect, allied to the extra work and timber needed to produce a shapely cabriole, doubtless played its part in driving the cabriole right out of the Windsor fashion. When that happened is anybody's guess. I should have said at some late date in the eighteenth century, were it not that in the Parker-Knoll Collection at High Wycombe there is a well-formed comb-back Windsor, with vase-splat and cabriole legs, of good style and quality, bearing beneath its seat the mutilated remains of an old hand-written maker's label, listing a variety of items. The words ' . . . Garden/ . . . Close Stools/ . . . tree or Beach Chair[s and St]ools/ . . . Made and Sold by/[?] Geo: . . ./Beaconsfield', are still decipherable. I can make nothing of the surname, but a modern label records that the 'set of ten chairs and two stools' was made by Arding & Son, Chair Manufacturers, Beaconsfield, in 1810; and that this information formerly appeared on the old label. This date, despite a certain 'dumpiness' and lack of subtlety in the cresting, is later than I should have cared to put to the chair, were it judged solely 'on style', but, as there is no cause to doubt the information, it follows that some cabriole Windsors may be more recent in origin than their mode suggests. One is here speaking of antique cabrioles—the type has been revived in more modern times—but when the overdue change of taste which originally demoted the cabriole took effect, all the makers of Windsors had to do was to revert to the turned leg, which, though the style of turning may itself have varied, had never gone out of use.

IV

It is after the middle of the eighteenth century that we begin to meet the so-called 'Chippendale Windsors': a label with as little justification as well can be. There is and presumably never was a 'Chippendale Windsor' in the same sense that we may have a 'Goodchild Windsor'. Almost the sole excuse for the former term is that the chairs concerned approximate in date or in some vague manner to a style prevalent in the 'Chippendale Period'—if, indeed, there was a Chippendale Period in fact. Though Thomas Chippendale (1718-1779) and his firm were important craftsmen of a consequence which has been somewhat unduly disparaged by a section of modern criticism, they were certainly not the only birds of note on the furniture-tree; and it is as plain as a pikestaff that their name has been applied to an enormous mass of furniture without any shadow of warranty. Indeed, it is the laxity with which their name has been accredited to hundreds and thousands of pieces they could not possibly have made that has been responsible for a revulsion of critical feeling against a firm of genuine merit and importance. There are signs that this attitude is giving place to a more generous, if still scholarly, appreciation, very different from the old, unreasoning enthusiasm which saw 'Chippendale' in everything that happened to be neither 'Hepplewhite' nor 'Sheraton'. Commercially, however, the 'Chippendale' label has still a wealth of life in it.

'Chippendale' is a good-sounding word, and makes for sales-talk, though the best-informed dealers use it with a decent discretion. It has, too, an advantage as giving a 'short-hand' indication of style and period; but beyond that it is all too often meaningless. Chippendale (let us say) made some Gothick chairs, therefore Gothick Windsors are 'Chippendale'. Again, possibly a splat has at some time reminded somebody of a Chippendale splat. *Ergo*, the Windsor splat is 'Chippendale'. Put thus, such propositions sound pretty feeble, but, once fairly stuck, labels like 'Chippendale' (or for that matter 'Goldsmith') are the deuce to detach.

Be it therefore understood that any future allusion to 'Chippendale' in this book implies no more than a stylistic allusion of a rough-and-ready order. It does *not* imply that the Windsor or Windsor-part concerned was made by the worthy Thomas Chippendale himself.

V

For the most part, this so-called 'Chippendale' influence—far less an expression of personality than of a period—this influence is seen in the design of Windsor-splats which now became fancifully and pleasingly perforated (*e.g.* Pls. 9, 12, 24, etc.). Hitherto, ornamentation of splats had been limited to linear effects, such as the vase- or classical baluster-outline (*e.g.* Pls. 10 and 13), as well as some others, but it should be emphasized that the presence of an unpierced, baluster-type splat is not, *per se*, indication of an Early Windsor. Alongside the so-called 'Chippendale' splats, the unpierced variety continued in production in the second half of the eighteenth century, either because of an innate conservatism in the making of Windsors, or because such chairs found a ready market among folk who preferred the older method. Besides which, the relative simplicity of cutting a solid splat as compared with one more or less elaborately pierced, doubtless recommended itself on grounds of technical economy. Whatever the reason in any given instance, it is, however, plain that though the unpierced baluster is more consonant in design with the earlier part of the eighteenth century, and often has a decidedly 'Queen Anne' appearance, it was not in fact abandoned until somewhere about the end of the century.

But the 'Chippendale' manner (still so to call it) had a more noticeable effect in the fashion of the elaborate 'Gothick' Windsors already mentioned in passing. Pls. 22 and 23 give their characteristics. Chairs of this type belong to the second half of the eighteenth century, perhaps especially from about 1770 (some say 1760) onwards, but it must be insisted that these are provisional dates and that modern renderings exist, including the remarkably fine recensions by 'Jack' Goodchild.

As apart from their Gothick trimmings, these chairs present two noteworthy details of construction. Their backs are stickless, support being ensured by one 'through' splat supplemented by a system of minor ones, all these providing the material for the Gothick shapes and perforations of that type of Gothick known variously as 'Strawberry Hill', 'Twickenham', or 'Jemmy'—the two former terms suggested by 'Horry' Walpole's

mediaevalized home at Twickenham. The backs are bowed, some, such
as those in Pl. 23, being the more Gothick in effect by being built up of
two bows joined at an acute angle at the top. A simpler type of one-piece
bow is, however, seen on other examples, as in Pl. 22. An interesting
variant, noted in *Antiques* (September 1952, p. 215) by Mr David Stockwell, occurs in a pair of old American Windsors *combining* the arch-
and bow-back, the arch (*within* the bow) being filled not with a splat but
ladder-wise.

This does not mean that all Gothick Windsors have stickless backs.
On some, the splat alone may reveal a Gothick pretension, as in Pl. 25,
or more conspicuously in Pl. 21, where the splat, though of common type
as to its lower part, swells at the top into the semblance of a Gothic
window, though in other respects the build is that of a normal bow-back
of the late eighteenth century. A more refined treatment of this 'window-
splat' is seen on a fan-back Windsor of yew and beech, with shaped cresting, in the Victoria and Albert Museum (W. 8–1949), where, incidentally,
it is assigned to the mid-eighteenth century, though, perhaps, second
half of the eighteenth century would be a preferable approximation.
'Window-splats' (so to call them) are found in degrees of degeneration
from the Gothick, some being scarcely recognizable as 'windows' at all
unless one happens to know the origin of the design.

Besides 'window-splats' and other chairs with semi-Gothick splats,
one meets less elaborate chairs to which the term 'Gothick' is not in-
appropriate, though the taste here is not 'Chippendale' but (again in a
broad usage) 'Regency'. Of such is the 'Interlaced Bow' type of bow-back
(Pl. 32). Presumably originating in the late eighteenth or early nineteenth
century, this attractive pattern was a Windsor adaptation of an interlaced
tracery found on superior chair-backs of non-Windsor build and of
'Sheraton' period. To craftsmen now thinking largely in terms of bows,
the form was easily translated in terms of Windsor technique. 'Interlaced
Bows' were still in the makers' catalogues of the 1850's or '60's, and
modern recensions are known. Despite its completely Regency air, the
charming example in Pl. 32 was made by Mr T. C. Sutton about 1910,
and even later examples are found. Still more attractive is the related type
of bow-back in Pl. 33, itself a Windsor variant of a known design. I have
heard of one more or less modern bow-back of which the interlaced fillings
were said to have been supplied by broken bows, which were thus very
satisfactorily used up, though I am far from suggesting that all Interlaced
Bows or related types were made—in part—of remnants. Doubtless
lesser bows were specially bent for the purpose.

Be it said here that though 'Regency' is as much a stylistic label as 'Chippendale', as far as Windsors are concerned, its use has more to recommend it. Just as one speaks (if one must) of 'Chippendale' Windsors, so one finds mention of 'Hepplewhite' and 'Sheraton' Windsors, though it need not be idly supposed that the firms of Hepplewhite or of Sheraton were directly implicated. When it seems necessary to·use these popular descriptions, their use will not be shirked in these pages. On stylistic grounds, they have an occasional reality transcending that of the 'Chippendale' myth, though in general they are best left alone. On the other hand, 'Regency', however much it overlaps the historical Regency of 'Prinney', is an embracing stylistic term which need not be twisted out of decency. We shall have reason to use it again.

VI

Though special attention is the due of the Gothick types, it should not be supposed that they were characteristic of the general output of Windsors in the second half of the eighteenth century. If the present scarcity of antique Windsors of the elaborate Gothick sort may be partly attributable to wastage by wear and tear, it also seems possible that they were to some extent regarded as eccentric and that, accordingly, the original output was relatively low. This (to stress the point) would apply much more to chairs like those in Pls. 22 and 23, than to simpler varieties, or to chairs in which the Gothick taste was limited to semi-Gothic perforations of the splat; though even in the case of such semi-persistent types as the Interlaced Bow, it would not seem that extensive quantities of any antiquity have survived. Rather, the main tendency was to adhere to types of Windsor which were either already traditional or in process of becoming so. The cabriole leg seems to have been abandoned not long after the close of the century, giving place, except in modern revivals, for the wholesale readoption of the turned leg, which, as has been shown, had never died out; and though backs were made increasingly on the bow principle, chairs of comb-back type, though usually with splats, were still produced.

Thus, carried over into the early part of the nineteenth century,·we find chairs which, apart from lesser details, conform with the comb-backs or bow-backs of the previous age. These, as well as later developments, will be discussed in due order. Before doing so, however, we may as well note one or two abnormalities in the way of Windsors made of mahogany:

a wood which, though not very well suited to the Windsor technique and but rarely used in it, occasionally gave birth to a noteworthy item. It may be suspected that mahogany Windsors were on the whole produced to special order, or in some instances as show-pieces demonstrating what the maker could do in a fashionable wood. So rare and finely finished a type as the Windsor in Pl. 26 would not be much repeated, though, I fancy, it has been *copied*.

A point to be noted in this elegant chair is the delicate carving of the pierced splat with wheat-ears, husks, rosettes, a swag and scrolling in the classical taste of the end of the eighteenth century, which, though common on other furniture, is extremely rare on Windsors. Another detail of interest is the provision of cross-stretchers on the X-principle, instead of the average Windsor ties.

A more conventional type of Windsor, also in mahogany, with bow-back, sticks, and cabrioles, of an average type of mid- to second half of the eighteenth century, is figured in Messrs M. Harris and Sons' book on *The English Chair* (1946, p. 128).

Completely different in almost every respect is a Windsor assigned to *circa* 1760-70, and at one time in the possession of the poet Cowper. This, as already noted, is now in the Victoria and Albert Museum, to which it was given by Mr H. J. Tait (W. 21-1933).[28] Solidly built, this chair enjoys the sumptuousness of an all but complete austerity, its unstretchered legs being of square section with small brackets, and the plain stick-back having a shaped cresting of a 'depressed-arch' formation which can be traced back to the 'humps-and-hollow' of non-Windsor chairs in general fashion some decades earlier—a shape to which the term 'Queen Anne' is freely, if too loosely, given. For the occupant's greater comfort, the elegantly shaped arms are broadened, a feature sometimes found on other Windsors, even in the eighteenth century though more numerously later; but though the top of the back is reminiscent of an earlier style than that generally current in 1760-70, this merely affords another instance of the tendency of the craftsmen of Windsors to look backward rather than forward.

I have called this Cowper Chair austere, and such is the initial impression received of a piece which persuades approval by its sheer simplicity and goodness. If unusual, it is in no wise eccentric, which is more than can be said for an extremely unorthodox Windsor (not of mahogany) known to me from a photograph. This is basically a low stick-back of perhaps the end of the eighteenth century, but on the arm-bow is imposed a head-rest consisting of a narrow recurved bow forming an open loop, filled with a shaped splat, both ends of which are arrow-headed. Assuming this to be a homogeneous piece, it is certainly rare, and is in any case a type outside the normal run of Windsors.

VII

As we approach the 'Regency', new influences become apparent, at first in such details as the piercing of splats, or in a tendency, already seen in certain Gothick Windsors, to multiply splats, sometimes with distinctly pleasing results, as in Pl. 37. The fashion for triple-splat backs, with or without sticks as well, appears late in the eighteenth century, and carries on well into the nineteenth, when, by the way, a dual-splat type with 'tablet' top is grimly figured in Glenister & Gibbons' lithographed pattern-book. Old triple-splats are not now common (Pls. 34, 38), though modern recensions exist. In passing, it may be noted that a bow-back Windsor with shaped and perforated triple splats augmented by sticks, and its underframing secured by a double cow-horn stretcher, is seen in a drawing of the vestry of 'Little Dorrit's Church'—in other words St George the Martyr, Southwark—reproduced some forty or fifty years ago in the old *Daily Graphic*.

As Regency ideas bit deep into the Windsor complex, these resulted in the eventual adoption of an altogether simpler type of back. Before discussing the latter development, let us note the tendency to pierce the upper end of the splat with such motifs as a classical urn, or the 'Prince of Wales' Feathers'—to give that royal badge its popular description (Pls. 28, 36, 38).

These attractive embellishments arrived no earlier than the very close of the eighteenth century, and survived into the nineteenth. In the *plumes d'ostruce* Badge for Peace of the Heir Apparent, we have an obvious allusion to the 'First Gentleman in Europe', George Prince of Wales, the Prince Regent for whom the Regency Style is loosely named, and who as King George IV reigned from 1820 to his death in 1830. This 'Feathers' *motif* is said to have been borrowed by the makers of Windsors from a favourite device of the firm of Hepplewhite, appointed Chair-makers to 'Prinney', as the Prince was called by his intimates. The device is patriotic, and, though its derivation from Hepplewhite is plausible, it must be noted that chairs with 'Feathers' in their backs were made by other firms. Indeed, no great imaginative effort would be needed to arrive at a device so freely distributed.

Whether 'Feathers' Windsors survived the Regency, or the longer period of the First Gentleman's career as Prince of Wales (to which they properly refer) is unknown to me. Logically, the device would have become meaningless on his succession to the Throne in 1820, though it may have endured for a while as a decorative habit. None of the 'Feathers' Windsors known to me suggests a late survival, and I have yet to discover evidence for a revival of the device on Windsors when the next Prince of Wales (later King Edward VII) was born in 1841. Besides occurring on single-splat chairs of this type, the 'Feathers' device is found, somewhat rarely, on chairs of triple-splat build. Whilst on the subject of patriotic devices, let us note the occurrence of chairs of early nineteenth-century build on which the splat is pierced with a Crown. There is no confusing these with such an early eighteenth-century chair as that discussed in Chapter III, Section II. In build and character they are distinct, and the crowns are differently treated. That old 'crown-splat' Windsors of nineteenth-century fashion are now rare is perhaps not necessarily an indication of their original unpopularity. King George III's Jubilee (1809), and the coronations of George IV (1821), William IV (1831), and just possibly Queen Victoria (1838), suggest times at which such chairs might have been in demand.

'Feathers' chairs are now among the most desired types of antique Windsors, though the 'Urn-splat' can be equally attractive (Pl. 29). I call this pierced device an urn, though in some cases its character is indeterminate, suggestive of a floral (tulip) form, or an inverted husk of a classical type—all shapes which would tend to blend together in the hands of rural benchmen. As classical urns were popular in late eighteenth and early nineteenth-century design, there is no harm in seeing in the piercing of certain of these splats a formalized urn with lugs and a beknobbed or flaming cover; but that such a device was either blended into, or replaced by, actual floral forms is shown by the piercing of the splat of such a nineteenth-century lath-back Windsor as one now in the lounge of 'The Crown' at Chinnor, Oxon—a chair quite probably of Wycombe make.

It will be noticed that the chairs discussed in detail in this sub-section are, apart from their splats, of stick-back type, either crested or with bows, and that, especially in the former, the traditional element is strong.

VIII

About the time that these chairs—'Feathers' and related types—were making an initial appearance, one also first encounters a Windsor which

was long to outlive them—that type known as the 'wheel-back', or
more precisely the 'wheel-splat' Windsor (*e.g.* Pl. 30), of which more
than one variety exists. As this chair, though common, is of unusual
interest as having been made without a break ever since somewhere
about the junction of the eighteenth and nineteenth centuries, its origin
is worth consideration.

A rear view of what looks like a related type of chair, with bow-back
and a splat with vertical perforations and a spokeless circular opening,
is conspicuous in the well-known engraving of *The Visit Returned in the
Country*, by W. Nutter after George Morland, published by W. Dickinson,
1 May, 1789.[29] Morland was casual over details, which may be a reason
why the old farmer's chair in this composition looks a shade uncon-
vincing. For our purpose, however, the occurrence of this countrified
chair at least suggests an approach to the 'wheel' Windsor, since become
so familiar to us.

It is to be noted that fashionable chair-design of roughly the same date
as Nutter's engraving not infrequently exhibits a circular back, provided
with a somewhat similar if more elegant splat, embellished at its central
point with a device resembling a rosette, or patera, pierced spokewise. A
good example of this is a stylish mahogany chair assigned to *circa* 1785,
in the Victoria and Albert Museum (W. 68-1935).[30] Other examples or
varieties could be cited but this is enough for our purpose, and it is at
least arguable that the Windsor 'wheel' was evolved from some such
examplar. Your town designer or craftsman might think in terms of a
perforated rosette of classical temper, but to the country mind spokes were
spokes and a wheel was a wheel; and as such it figured in the wheel-splat
Windsor.

Sometimes the wheel-*motif* is modified to an encircled cross (Pl. 36a),
though whether this necessarily had a religious significance is another
matter. Macquoid and Edwards' *Dictionary of English Furniture* illustrates
a child's high-chair (Fig. 112 in Vol. I of that book), of which the circular
space is filled with a six-rayed star, its points overlapping the circumference
of the circle.[31] Yet another circular device is a turned, unperforated boss,
found on both single- and triple-splat chairs, the boss occupying the same
position on the splat as the 'wheel', and perhaps adopted as an improve-
ment on it, as I think it arrived on Windsors at a somewhat later date
(Pl. 34). This boss is again derived, at sundry removes, from classical
sources, and is of course common on other forms of woodwork. For a
time, at any rate, it was frequently used on Windsors, but, though it had
a long innings, it did not out-last the 'wheel', which has maintained a

permanent place in the Windsor repertory. Indeed, the 'wheel' is one of the most satisfactory forms of Windsor yet evolved, and just how well it responds to a master-touch is seen in an example made in recent years by Goodchild (Pl. 52). It would be possible to write a good deal about the original prices of this or that form of Windsor, but all I shall do here is to add that Alderman Janes recalls a day when half a dozen good wheel-splat Windsors would be had for twelve shillings and sixpence! Not that this was always the case, nor is it so any longer.

When such chairs as these are spoken of as showing 'Hepplewhite' influence, it is with scarcely more validity than graces the ascription of 'Chippendale' to their forerunners.

IX

Meanwhile, the so-called 'Chippendale' splat was coarsening into forms suggestive of the onset of Victorianism. The process was not everywhere the same, as there is no reason whatever to suppose that splats of purely eighteenth-century design ceased to be made in at any rate the first half of the nineteenth, and many cases occur in which the actual date of a chair embodying such splats can only be decided by the character of other details. Thus, whereas some splats of eighteenth-century design or derivation display significant attenuation, suggestive of a lapsing enthusiasm, others become coarsened until the eighteenth-century character is either all but lost, or else acquires a fussiness in some wise suggestive of Berlin Woolwork.

It is customary to speak of the last variety as 'Yorkshire' or 'Lancashire' Windsors (see Pls. 39 and 40), though it would be unwise to insist on those shires as their place of origin in every instance. Reference to old pattern-books shows that equivalent types were in production at High Wycombe by at any rate the middle of the nineteenth century, but that such showy Windsors were popular in the northern provinces is allowable. Apart from the occurrence of these chairs in such parts of England (not of itself an absolute test), a taste for such elaborate decorative treatment finds an analogy in the development of the long-case clock, which in Yorkshire, Lancashire, and other northern centres tended to be not only broader in the beam but more elaborately decorated than its southern counterparts. For all I know to the contrary, an undulating line from Norfolk to the Bristol Channel might very roughly indicate the respective spheres of influence, though no positive demarcation is allowable. As far as clocks are concerned, the business-like northerner's desire to obtain full value for his expenditure of 'brass', coupled with the rise of 'new men' of the successful-industrialist class, goes far to explain this preference for showily-cased clocks, not always in the best of taste; and that like considerations affected the design of Windsors is at least arguable.

This northern addiction to large and pretentious long-case clocks becomes apparent in the late eighteenth century, to which same period are assigned at any rate some of the 'Yorkshire' and 'Lancashire' Windsors, though most of the latter which I have seen are more suggestive of the first half of the nineteenth. For one thing, many of them exhibit legs and stretchers boldly turned in heavy patterns dissimilar from the slender turnings typical of the eighteenth century. If some of the best of these chairs date from anywhere between the 1820's and 1840's, in which latter decade numerous types of heavy-legged chairs occur, I should not be surprised. It is, moreover, evident that, in the south as well, heavy turnings were popular in the 1850's and '60's. Windsors with markedly bulbous turnings, and incorporating cup-like shapes allied to those in so-called 'trumpet-turning', can be normally attributed to about that period, when a tendency to a 'sausage' turning with a double, instead of a single 'swell' is also encountered (Pl. 43). Mr Symonds has noted that what he terms Lancashire Windsors are generally of yew throughout, except for the elm-wood seat.

On the other hand, it is evident that simpler turnings, of an elegance recalling the late eighteenth or early nineteenth centuries, were not abandoned, and though some of the Windsor legs in Walter Skull's designs of 1849 show a marked tendency to elaboration, the older, slender type was not forgotten, and was in course of time to win the day by a sheer simplicity for which we may be thankful. Comparison of the legs in Pls. 37, 39, 40, 50, 51, will give some indication of the march to a grossness which defeated itself by its own exuberance, but which, whatever its failings, was far from devoid of character.

X

Meanwhile, the traditional Windsor types had been seriously threatened by an adaptation of the back on lines borrowed, in the main, from Regency models. To a first glance, this change seems so revolutionary as to cancel all that went before it, though in fact a certain continuity is discernible.

Pl. 26. Late eighteenth-century mahogany bow-back, notable for its splat which, besides its pierced work, is delicately carved with wheat-ears, husks, rosettes, a swag, and scrolling in the classical taste of the period.

Pl. 27. Comb-back chair of slightly 'fan' type. Late eighteenth century.

Pl. 28. This late edition of fan-back displays the 'Prince of Wales' Feathers'.

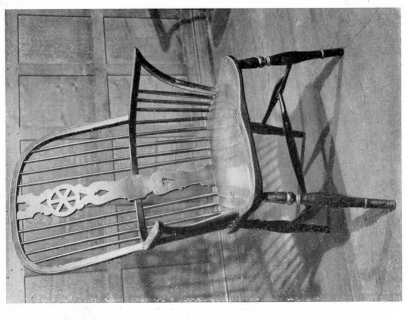

Pl. 29. Contemporaneously with the 'Feathers' type
(Pls. 28, 36, 38), similar Windsors have splats pierced

Pl. 30. Best-known of all English Windsors is the 'Wheel-
splat' type of bow-back.

Pl. 31. The Pine Kitchen at the Henry Francis du Pont Winterthur Museum, Delaware, showing American Windsors with continuous back-and-arm bows, and turnings of 'Rhode Island' type.

Pls. 32, 33, 34, 35. *Above left:* 'Interlaced Bow', a modified 'Gothick' type of Windsor originating in the late eighteenth-early nineteenth century, or under Regency influence. *Above right:* Related to the 'Interlaced Bow' (Pl. 32) and originating in a like period is this attractive late-type, bow-back Windsor *c.* 1910. *Below left:* Triple-splat Windsor showing so-called 'Hepplewhite' influence *c.* 1840. *Below right:* Simple fan-back Windsor with undished circular seat. Descendant of a mid-eighteenth century type, of which quite modern examples are found.

Pl. 36 a & b. Children's High Chairs of types belonging to the earlier part of the nineteenth century.

Pls. 37, 38, 39, 40. *Above left:* Elegant bow-back Windsor with triple-splat formation and unusually neat finish of the arm-tops and bases of arm-supports. *Above right:* Unusual triple-splat Windsor of 'Prince of Wales' Feathers' type, the device being repeated in the small side-splats supporting the arms. *Below:* Bow-back Windsors of 'Yorkshire' or 'Lancashire' type.

Pl. 41. 'Mendlesham Chair', by Daniel and Richard Day, of Mendlesham, Suffolk.
Early nineteenth century.

Pls. 42, 43, 44, 45. *Above left:* 'Tablet-top' Windsor of Regency style, but assigned to *c.* 1840. *Above right:* 'Lath and Baluster' Windsor of beech with elm seat, and double cross-stretcher—nineteenth century. *Below:* Two of many varieties of 'Scroll' Windsors which carried the 'Regency' tradition well into the nineteenth century.

Pl. 46. Red-stained 'Smoker's Bow' in a style of about the mid-nineteenth century and with more elegant turnery than appears on later examples.

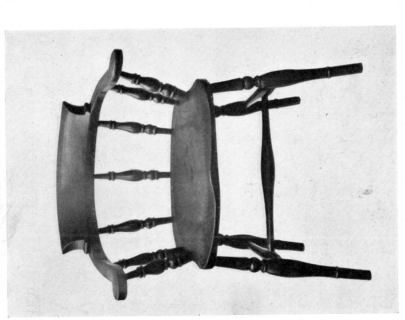

Pl. 47. Berger (bergère) Bow Windsor, with shaped back and arms in three pieces c. 1850-65.

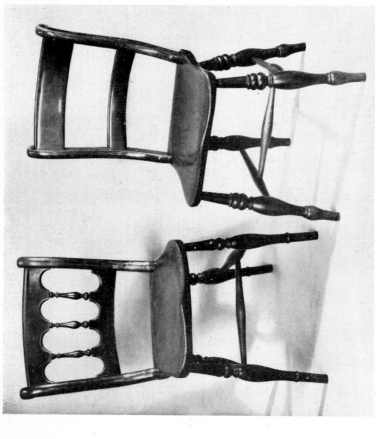

Pl. 49 a & b. *Left*: 'Gothic Spindle' Windsor, with turned spindles in the back, of a type originating in the first half of the nineteenth century. *Right*: The commonest of all the many types of 'Scroll' Windsor, of beech with elm seat.

Pl. 48. Three-legged Windsor stool, *c.* 1870.

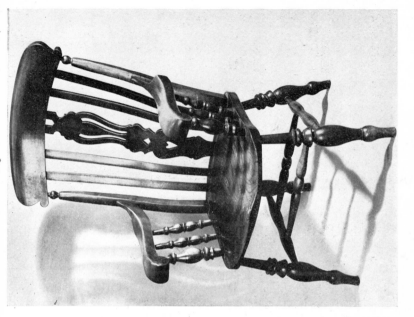

Pl. 51. Typical Wycombe lath-and-baluster Windsor in beech, stained red and varnished.

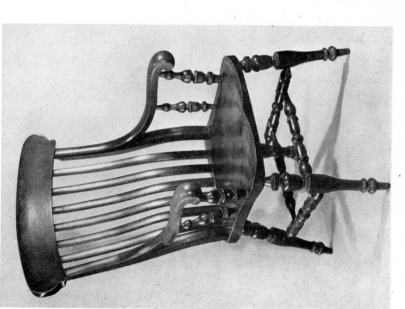

Pl. 50. Wycombe lath-back Windsor in beech, stained red and varnished to imitate rose-wood or mahogany.

Pl. 52. A 'Goodchild Windsor', by H. E. ('Jack') Goodchild (1885-1950), of
Naphill, near High Wycombe, Bucks.

Pl. 53. Interior of 'Jack' Goodchild's workshop at Naphill, Bucks, with Windsors in various stages of manufacture.

Pl. 34 'Jack' (Harold Edward Goodchild (1885–1950)) filing a Gothick splat in his workshop at Naphill, Bucks

This especially applies to the traditional seating and under-framing of the chair, on which in effect a new type of back is imposed, bow and stick-filling being replaced by uprights, technically 'stands', linked by a top-rail and midway back-rest. In some designs, this top-rail is a cresting allied in principle to the earlier comb-cresting, in others the rail is set between, and not across, the 'stands' or uprights. The 'Tablet-top', of which a relatively early example is seen in Pl. 42, is an instance of the former, and it will be noticed that the tendency in this and allied construction is to a deep cresting; a tendency which had already reached exaggerated proportions by 1823, in which year Wilkie painted the 'Grand Old Duke of York' seated in a non-Windsor chair of such a type.[32] Similar non-Windsor chairs are profusely present in the illustrations to that good old classic *The Adventures of Mr Verdant Green*, by 'Cuthbert Bede' (The Rev. Edward Bradley), originally published in 1853-56. But if (on Windsors) the cresting had changed, the basic principle of chairs so fashioned remained unaltered. Moreover, the continuance of types approximating to the comb-back, but with a filling of either sticks or laths, and, not infrequently, with splats of semi-eighteenth century design, preserved that much more of the old idea from oblivion. Nor is there cause to suppose that traditional types of plain stick or wheel-splat bow-backs ceased to be made.

This is clearly shown at High Wycombe Public Library by a large coloured lithographic broadsheet issued as a pattern-book by Edwin Skull of High Wycombe, and printed by Alfred Reeves & Co., Falcon Steam Works, Finsbury Street, London, at some time after October 1865, which date appears on it as that of a certificate of merit presented by the Earl of Carnarvon in connection with an exhibition at Reading Town Hall. Among the numerous tiny illustrations of chairs on this broadsheet are various Windsors, including wheel-splat, scroll, and Smoker's-Bow types, but most impressive is one of a tall bow-back armchair, with sticks and splat, which might almost pass for a late eighteenth- early nineteenth-century piece. Here is clear evidence that even in the later 1860's a Georgian type of Windsor was still in commercial production.

Some of the newer types of chair in which the comb-back principle was in essence retained may be mentioned, those known as 'Stick-back', 'Lath-back', 'Roman spindle', 'Baluster-and-Spindle', and 'Lath-and-Baluster' (Pl. 43). 'Stick-back' was here a carry-over from an older type, 'Lath-back' being similar, but with laths instead of sticks. In 'Baluster-and-spindle' we have an instance of the use of the word baluster [or may

E

be banister] for splat, as generally employed by the makers of Windsors, including 'Jack' Goodchild himself.

In the case of Pl. 43, the decadent splat invites comparison with one on a bow-back Windsor as illustrated in J. C. Loudon's *Encyclopædia of Cottage, Farm, and Villa Architecture and Furniture*, originally published in 1833, and re-issued in 1842 and 1857. Though dissimilar in detail, the splats are clearly allied in character; and, while on the subject of Pl. 43, we may as well notice that its underframing shows the use of the double stretcher which had something of a vogue about the middle and the third quarter of the nineteenth century, though Mr F. H. Glenister has told me that he has an impression that it was a mark of 'better' Windsors. It is, moreover, noteworthy that in the Thomas Glenister album of drawings, one of an ordinary Smoker's Bow has a pencilled alteration adapting it to double-stretcher construction.

Chairs of these various types were produced in quantity and still abound in the Chilterns, the most noticeable of them being capacious armchairs which, despite their heavy build, can be surprisingly comfortable in use (Pls. 50 and 51). A typical Windsor of this sort, now in High Wycombe Museum, to which it was given by Miss L. Lord, was made by Mr More of West End Road in that town, but such chairs were turned out in large quantities by many makers from somewhere about the middle third to the last third of the nineteenth century and even later. It is thus quite feasible for a plain lath-back in the style of, say, the 1840's to have been made as late as the junction of the nineteenth and twentieth centuries. If less appealing to the eye than the more traditional types, the curving and angling of the laths to support the back of an occupant is often adjudged with a scientific nicety. It is quite possible to use these chairs without recourse to cushions, and to be at one's ease, which, to be candid, is not always so when eighteenth-century Windsors are concerned. Such chairs, with legs of a faceted conic section not unsuggestive of loosely furled umbrellas, or with legs exhibiting the bold turning and cup-like members previously noticed, are indicative of a response to styles of the 1840's, '50's, '60's, or later, for here, as almost always when Windsors are in question, cautious estimation is desirable.

One of the most noteworthy details in the design of such chairs is the opportunity afforded by many of them for us to trace the decadence of the eighteenth-century splat, still in some sort surviving more than half a century after it had ceased to be modish (Pls. 43 and 51). Though these solidly built and comfortable chairs are not as yet much esteemed by critical collectors, they have their place in the pedigree of Windsors and—let me whisper it—such of them as are not yet accounted 'genuine antiques' are on their way to that haven of guaranteed respectability. Even so, it is a counsel of caution not to assume too lightly that all examples are as old as the somewhat vague dates I have mentioned. Once established, the type had its life.

Another Victorian innovation which, if none too sightly, was both useful and comfortable, is the 'Berger Bow'—no self-respecting maker of Windsors would have dreamed of calling it *bergère*—of which a characteristic example, probably by Daniel Glenister of High Wycombe, is seen in Pl. 47. Though Bergers are indebted to the more conventional *bergère* form, as known a good deal earlier in non-Windsor types, they are also related to the Windsor Corner-Chair called Smoker's or Smoker Bow, as already mentioned (*e.g.* Pl. 46), of which quantities were made in the course of the century, some with the gouty turning suggestive of the '40's and '50's, others more slender and elegant, though not on that account necessarily earlier in date.

Among other forms of Windsor are Close-Chairs or Night-Commodes (such as are figured in Glenister & Gibbons's catalogue); and Rocking-Chairs occur among Walter Skull's designs of 1849, and those of other Wycombe makers of later date. Some of these last exhibit turnings of a kind borrowed from romantic furniture of quasi-antique or 'Abbotsford' character. One such Rocker, perhaps of the 1860's or later, known to me, is 'grained' in imitation of a superior wood, after a favoured fashion of the period, and it was certainly not the sole example of its kind. A like tendency to graining may be found on other types of Windsors of nineteenth-century date. The example is not one to be followed.

It is not suggested that either Close- or Rocking-Chair Windsors of better style were unknown at an earlier period. Doubtless both occurred in Windsor form in the eighteenth century; but, as more must be said about Rockers in Chapter IV, we may as well pass to a matter of immediate importance.

XI

It is high time to say more of the revolutionary change which replaced sticks and bow with top-rail and cross-bar in the backs of a huge number of Windsors. Of these, there are far more varieties than can be mentioned here, though in a general way those in which the 'stands' or uprights of the back scrolled over backwards were known as 'Scroll Chairs'—a term which I had from Goodchild himself.

Basically, the type is classical, of 'Regency' vintage, though here again the term is stylistic and far from necessarily datal. Scroll Chairs bridge the nineteenth century, being still made in recognizable forms long after any 'Regency' impulse had been forgotten (Pls. 44, 45, 49). Among variants of the Scroll, such a chair as that in Pl. 49 is mildly noteworthy, its trade-name, 'Gothic Spindle', being dimly justified by the arched openings and turned spindles in the upper part of the back. Such chairs are noteworthy as Windsor emulations of a type of back popular on other forms of Victorian seating, among them gilt non-Windsor chairs for 'rout' or drawing-room usage. It is noticeable that the Windsor version remains stubbornly *sui generis* as regards its seat and under-framing, for however much the backs of such later Windsors were revolutionized, the method of plugging the 'stands' into the seats, the seats themselves, and the character of the under-framing remained obstinately 'Windsor'.

Whereas the cresting of lath-back and allied Windsors is sometimes curved at the ends in a manner suggestive of numerous non-Windsor types, Scroll Chairs are necessarily blunt-ended for tenoning into the uprights. A 'bridge' between the two types is suggested by the Scroll Windsor in Fig. 44, of which the top-rail is incised with lines simulating curving. As used, such incised work, found also on non-Windsors, is merely an uncertain grace-note.

XII

To all intents and purposes, the Victorian era saw nearly the last of many developments of the Windsor Chair, save in respect of such a mid-nine-teenth-century indiscretion as the attempt, already mentioned, to com-bine the Windsor and cane-back or Windsor and cane-seat types in one inharmonious chair; and saving a revival of sorts of the 'Goldsmith' Windsor under aesthetic influence towards the century's close.[33] One recalls, too, the black-and-white advertisement of the firm of Norman & Stacey Ltd, of Tottenham Court Road, in use about the turn of the century, flatly designed with a Georgian gentleman and lady quizzing a Windsor-type comb-back, suspended in a Beardsleyan gloom. This chair, by the way, is represented as having a pronouncedly curved back, as, indeed, is sometimes found on antique examples.

Apart from these and such as these, no marked alteration of traditional design has, to my knowledge, been seen in our time, though an exception must be made in favour of that mid-twentieth century departure, the

'Ercol' Windsor Tub Chair made by Furniture Industries Ltd, High Wycombe. This Tub Windsor includes certain unfamiliar features, including a cable-sprung frame and a spring-filled cushion in place of the old wooden seat; but, though this can rightly claim to be a new design,

Fig. IV. Extra-illustration, by Thomas Onwhyn, originally published 1837, for *Pickwick*.

the effect of a reasonable development of traditional methods has been carefully maintained. Be it emphasized that not all modern Windsors are thus seated. Wooden-seated Windsors are still made in profusion.

Naturally, there is no reason whatsoever why new patterns of Windsors should not arise as they have done, time and again, in the past. Provided that they be designed on sound and harmonious lines, they can but keep the craft from degenerating into a dull repetitiveness. That some modern bow-backs at any rate, have, to my eye, a short and stumpy look may be attributed as much to a certain loss of subtlety in their curves as to any other factor. To recapture that subtlety, so evident in many older Windsors, should not be beyond the power of modern mechanization.

As to miniature or toy Windsors, though many exist, the great majority are of modern or even of recent origin. If not unknown, toy Windsors of any antiquity are scarce to the point of rarity, so far as my experience goes.

XIII

A word about Windsor Stools, though scarcely more than a word. Desirable examples are rare, and not every one is old, though they have their prototypes in the rough stools, sometimes with three legs and circular seats, which abounded almost everywhere, and of which a typical instance occurs in Adriaen van Ostade's painting of *The Alchymist*, dated 1661, in the National Gallery, London (846). Other and earlier instances could be cited; but as to Windsor stools, one of the most attractive I have seen, beautifully built in the style of the second half of the eighteenth century, gave a good idea of the possibilities and presumably reflected an antique design, including a cabriole front-leg. Stylistically, it represented the taste of about a century earlier than the far less stylish stool in Pl. 48, which reveals an altogether commoner if, in certain basic respects, an older type. It is, however, obviously nineteenth-century, and in High Wycombe Museum, to which it belongs, it is assigned to *circa* 1870. Here the top is plain circular, neither saddled nor dished, and the unpolished wood is painted black.

To say that this exhausts the limits of Windsor stool-design would be far from true. Old Windsor stools and foot-stools occur in America; and in England there are, for example, the saddle-seated or circular-topped stools on turned legs, as used in public-house bars and other places of refreshment or commerce (Text Fig. IV). It is as well to remember that such pieces are Windsors, whether or not their value is more than utilitarian.

XIV

We have seen that Windsor Chairs were made in various parts of Britain, though the Wycombe area is that best known as a centre of the craft. Somerset, Yorkshire, Lancashire, Sussex, the Cotswolds,[34] and London herself (which Mr Symonds in 1935 was inclined to regard as being, with Berks and Bucks, the original *locus*), are some of the more obvious parts. Wales, Scotland, Canada, Denmark* and (with a previously noted reservation) Holland, also come into the picture [*cf.* Chapter I, IV.]. Not that the presence of a Windsor in a certain place is by any means necessarily a guarantee that it was made there, though in divers cases such an assumption is permissible and even probable. What must be allowed for is that the export of Windsors is no new thing. We shall see in the next chapter how at any rate some English Windsors were sent as far afield as Colonial America, and in England the same process of distribution was in being. Alderman R. A. Janes has told me that his great-grandfather employed men to make chair-parts 'in the woods round Penn and Amersham as far back as 1780'. As there was then no (organized) production of chairs in Wycombe, such parts were 'sent to London and other towns, even as far away as Scotland'. As it is obviously easier to transport chair-parts than completed chairs (though the latter was certainly done), it may be assumed that a good deal was arranged in this way, though the advent of the railways would have greatly increased the facilities for transport of the finished article. As to how far London's contribution was actually local, or to what extent it relied on parts supplied from places like Wycombe, is a detail not easily assessed. In one way or another, it must have been extensive, and the following notice may be taken as typical: '// Stubbs's Manufactory, / in the City Road and in Brick Lane Old Street,/London./For all sorts of Yew Tree, Gothic and Windsor/Chairs Alcoves and Rural Seats Garden Machines/Dyed Chairs etc., on the most reasonable Terms//'.

Nevertheless, recognizable forms of locally fashioned Windsors are found, among which the distinctive varieties of Windsor or quasi-Windsor built in East Anglia demand our attention. These are known, not as Windsors, but as Scole or Mendlesham Chairs, from Scole in Norfolk and Mendlesham in Suffolk, which were either the centres or the main centres of their manufacture. The distinctions between such chairs and those of average Windsor type are such as fully to justify the retention of their individual names, but, for all that, the relation of Scole and Mendlesham chairs to the Windsor *genus* is so close as to warrant their inclusion in this book. It is probably just to say that both 'Scole' and

* 'Windsor chairs made of beech' were among the modern furniture, 'designed for F.D.B. (The Danish Co-operative Wholesale Society) by Börge Mogensen', in the Book-stall, Danish Art Treasures Exhibition, at the Victoria and Albert Museum, 1948-49 (*vide* Catalogue).

'Mendlesham' as terms are somewhat loosely applied, though the alternative name of 'Dan Day Chairs' for the Mendlesham variety enabled Mr Symonds to clarify the nebulous references made to them by other writers.

It appears that a local chair-maker of Mendlesham, Daniel Day, had a son who, 'about 1790 is said to have worked for Thomas Sheraton, afterwards returning to his father's workshop'.[25] Be it noted that the name is not recorded in any trade category in the Mendlesham section of William White's *History, Gazetteer, and Directory of Suffolk* (1844), though 'Day, Rev. Hy. Ts. L.L.D.' was then at the Vicarage. In the same compiler's volume on *Norfolk* (1836), we have better luck in finding, *sub* Scole, Thomas Rayner, joiner; and, in *Kelly's Directory* for 1904, one notices a Sidney Rayner, carpenter, in the same village.

In a letter (dated 3 April, 1950), Mr Edwin Gunn of Minehead informed me that Norfolk chairs with dished seats and simply reeded stick and splat backs, of a type 'which might be called "Farmhouse Hepplewhite"', could be bought for a few shillings apiece 'in remote un-tourist-haunted towns' like Downham Market 'as recently as 1923'; not that collectors need now be hopeful of securing examples at such a price-level.

Not a few of these chairs are of their kind attractive, and it is equally certain that the Mendlesham firm of Day—Dan and his son Richard—were craftsmen of more than average capability and good taste. The best of their work is among the best country-made furniture of its time. A glance at Pl. 41, showing a chair identical with one in Christchurch Mansion, Ipswich, gives a good idea of their quality. According to Mr Symonds,[36] 'Dan Day' chairs are usually of yew and fruitwood, with elm seats; the uprights and back-rails being inlaid with a box-wood line, just visible in Pl. 41. The pleasing proportions and interesting use of a decorative bow at the base of the back are worth noting, as are the nicely placed ball-ornaments, characteristic of Mendlesham chairs, though by no means uncommon on non-Windsor types, and so familiar to our eyes when snuggled into the hollows of Georgian mirror-frames.

CHAPTER IV

American Windsors

I

IF IN England the Windsor was usually a lower-to-middle-class chair—and, being but seldom politically conscious, I make no bones about so factual a definition—its use in America was even more thoroughly democratic. True, an American writer has called it 'appropriate to the porch, the kitchen, and the interior of the genuine farm-house', adding that 'its use in connexion with the better grade of furniture is a decorative error';[37] but, though this somewhat austere view may well have prevailed in modish circles even in the past, the fact remains that, in Colonial days, Windsors were used and esteemed by persons in widely differing grades of the community. If they were found in the backwoodsman's cabin, they had also a place of sorts on the average porch, or in the homes of the prominent. George Washington himself found a use for Windsors at Mount Vernon. Thomas Jefferson had a well-used comb-back armchair adapted to his personal needs by the addition of a swivel seat and a writing-flat, on which he is said to have drafted the Declaration of Independence, though precisely when these refinements were made is, perhaps, another matter.[38] Finally, sufficing a summary capable of much extension, we have in Ralph Earl's painting of *Roger Sherman*, circa 1775, not only a portrait of the grim-visaged shoemaker soon to be a signatory to the Declaration of Independence (1776), but a likeness of an American equivalent of the Smoker's Bow, rendered in accurate detail.[39] In face of these and many other direct associations, not least of them the use of Windsors at the signing of the Declaration itself, it cannot be felt that American Windsors are lacking in historical significance.

II

As in England, Windsors emerge fully fledged, though when they did so is again a problem on which opinion differs. A variety of dates from *circa* 1700 to as late as *circa* 1760 has been advanced, though the latter is demonstrably over-cautious. So far as existing knowledge takes us, somewhere about 1720-30 would seem to be a safe approximation, though the mass of surviving American Windsors is, perhaps, no earlier than the

second half of the eighteenth century. Even so, it is not my intention to
discuss the datal system as applied by certain American writers to individual Windsors: a system which has been worked out with loving care and
in considerable detail. To this I defer, though it has occasionally struck me
that either some few of the American datings are too early or some few
of the English datings are too late. I leave it at that, with the proviso that
the reference is not to documentary research, but to the assignment of
types of specimens on stylistic grounds. In any case, the care bestowed
by American critical opinion on the allocation and differentiation of local
types is as valuable as it is impressive.

How Windsors reached America is unknown, and unless the theory
of independent generation be accepted, there is an obvious temptation to
erect a pedigree from chairs brought over by settlers from the Old World.
Once seen by local craftsmen, such imports would soon be copied and,
suggesting a source of revenue, thus start native sources of manufacture.
Local makers would have seen no reason why they should not have a
finger in so promising a pie. Moreover, imported chairs would soon be
copied or repeated by settlers themselves who, like their brethren in the
English countryside, were competent to make their own furniture. So
much is reasonable speculation; but that actual importation *was* in fact
practised, if at a later date than that implied above, is obvious. According
to Carl Bridenbaugh, in 1767, John Biggard of Charles Town, turner,
'introduced local manufacture of Windsor chairs "as cheap as any imported" ';[40] and in September, 1757, George Washington ordered 'one
doz'n strong Chairs of about fifteen shillings price' to be sent from
England, enclosing exact measurements of the bottoms, and details of
'three different colours to suit the papers of three of the bed chambers'.[41]
It is generally assumed that these chairs were Windsors, as they doubtless
were, though the name itself is not used. Washington's purpose (not
devoid of economical ingenuity) was to transfer the bottoms (or seats)
of these imported chairs to certain American chairs, 'made in the Country
neat but too weak for common sitting', and to build two composite sets,
'for which reason the Workman must be very exact, neither making the
bottoms larger nor smaller . . . otherwise the change can't be made'.[41]
Such shifts as this align with an American tendency to convert Windsors
to individual requirements by the addition or substitution of parts: a
practical tendency, of which Thomas Jefferson's armchair at Philadelphia
is an outstanding instance.

Philadelphia claims the credit of having been the first American city
to produce Windsors, on, presumably, a commercial scale, and by at any

rate the first quarter of the eighteenth century, though once established the type was soon disseminated. 'Before 1750', says Carl Bridenbaugh, 'it was beginning to be widely used in taverns and public buildings'[42] though, says the same authority, it was not until 1774 that Windsors were made at New York—settees by John Ash, closely followed by chairs by John Kelso and Adam Galer.[42] *Per contra*, Thomas Hamilton Ormsbee cites an advertisement of 1765 by Andrew Gautier, a New Yorker of Huguenot parentage, this being illustrated by a crude cut of a comb-back Windsor of Philadelphia type.[43] Both Kelso and Galer had been apprenticed at Philadelphia[42], the reputed place of origin of the American Windsor and the cause of the term 'Philadelphia Chair', which (like 'Wycombe Chair' in England) need not be too narrowly interpreted. Thomas Jefferson's Windsor, already alluded to, is basically of Philadelphia type, its added writing-flat being matched by that attached to a more elegant comb-back, on which Emerson wrote *Nature*, and which, presumably, was anything but new when the great American writer thus immortalized it.[44] Writing-flats, and sundry forms of attached slides or even drawered or box-structures would seem to have been more appreciated on American Windsors than they ever were on their English counterparts (Pl. 11). In a number of cases, it is evident that such utilitarian devices, though old, are not coeval in date with the Windsors on which they occur.

As in England, the manufacture of Windsors spread beyond all hope of exact reckoning, city, township, hamlet, and isolated settlement alike contributing each its quota. No attempt can here be made to outline such a complex, still less to fill that outline with its multifarious detail. A rough-and-ready division of American Windsors into two 'schools', Philadelphia and New England, has been further sub-divided by investigators of the calibre of Ormsbee, who very properly pointed out that a Philadelphia type need not necessarily have been framed in that city.[45] As in England (where, for example, 'Yorkshire' or 'Lancashire' Windsors were not made solely in Yorkshire or Lancashire), both types and craftsmen might travel, taking their tradition with them.

III

Whereas English Windsors were more than sometimes painted, the American breed was quite frequently so finished, often in green, though other colours were also used. The main structural differences between the chairs is that the American makers eschewed the splat,[46] and set the legs nearer to the centre of the seat, splaying them at an acuter angle than was usual with the English product (Pls. 17 and 18). A tendency to prolong the curve of the back-bow forward, so as to take in the curve of the arms in one piece, instead of continuing it down to the seat and then adding the arms, is also noticeable in some late eighteenth- early nineteenth-century examples (Pl. 31). In certain instances the back-bow has a distinct 'waist'* in the lower part, and, in *Furniture Treasury*, Wallace Nutting illustrates a bow-chair with a serpentined top to the back. This he assigns, doubtless correctly, to *circa* 1800.

The pronounced leg-splay recently mentioned is, of course, an ancient method of construction, and could have been derived from English proto-types or from early true Windsors of English make, as a tendency to it is distinctly present in, say Pl 5, or in such a mid-eighteenth-century item as the Goldsmith Chair at South Kensington. It is, too, found in a phase of chairmaking on the European continent, reflected in American folk-craft by the Pennsylvania chairs with flat seats, and shaped backs cut from the solid plank, which are clearly influenced by continental European design. On balance, this constructional disposition of the legs may be an encouragement to such as claim a pre-1720 origin for the American Windsor, though it is not of itself proof of it. As a traditional form of construction, it retained its popularity in America, though it must not be supposed that splaying—and even acute splaying—was peculiar to that country!

Stick-back, comb-crested chairs, with legs either roughly hewn or neatly turned in various patterns, are also average constituents of early American Windsors, both high-back and low-back armchairs being found, the lower being of about the height of the English Smoker's Bow, though, at any rate in some instances, more capacious. The bow-back is also found in American Windsors of later type, being sometimes combined with the comb-back by a crested extension rising above the back-bow, and providing a tall head rest (Pls. 14, 15, 16). This superimposed comb, not unsuggestive of the 'Barber's Chair' (actual or so-called) in other types of furniture, is a striking and noteworthy feature, though the combination of bow and comb may not always achieve unity of design. A similar device is also found on some chairs other than bow-back Windsors.

* Bow-back Windsors with a pronounced 'waist' were not unknown in England. An armchair with a decided waist to its back occurs in an illustration, by an anonymous artist, to a serial story 'Echoes from the Belfry, by an Old Bell-Ringer', in an English periodical *Bow Bells: A Weekly Magazine of General Literature* (London: John Dicks, No. 141, Vol. VI N.S., 10 April 1867, p. 249). I am indebted to Mr George L. Suckling for bringing *Bow Bells* to my notice.

Shaping of seats, ranging from circular or elliptical to various forms of saddle outline, and various types of turning of legs and stretchers have been carefully noted by American students, enabling them to classify Windsors under such headings as Philadelphia, New England, Pennsylvania, Connecticut, Rhode Island, and Massachusetts. Indeed, far more attention has been paid to analyzing the technicalities of American Windsors than, in a connoisseur sense, has been given to the English. Diagrams illustrative of sundry patterns of seat and turning as used in America are given by Wallace Nutting, and by Thomas Hamilton Ormsbee. Among woods used for American Windsors are pine and whitewood, oak, ash, maple, birch, hickory, and, as in England, the all-walnut Windsor was not unknown. For what it is worth, we may as well note that when the American illustrator A. B. Frost was designing the plate '*All taps is vanities*', *replied Mr Stiggins*, for an edition of *Pickwick*, he chose to perch that unworthy 'shepherd' on a comb-back Windsor with turned legs of 'Connecticut' type. Without closely examining the divers styles of turning, we should at least note that the taste for 'bamboo' furniture, stimulated, though not initiated, in England by 'Prinney's' example at the Brighton Pavilion, had an influence on American turning for Windsors which cannot be matched on their English counterparts, though common enough on non-Windsor chairs of English make. 'Bamboo' turning on Windsors pre-dates the close of the eighteenth century in America, where it is found alongside other patterns, doubtless continuing well into the nineteenth. Be it added that though much bamboo-turning simulates the appearance of actual bamboo, the term is also loosely applied to shapes of a dimmer relationship.

Broadly speaking the earlier history of the American Windsor is that of the stick-back, developing from comb- or fan-back form with a somewhat simply shaped cresting, to a bow-back type, and on occasion combining both methods of construction.

An attempt to emulate a late-eighteenth-century round-back chair of 'Hepplewhite' type in Windsor technique, the main structure of the back being a circular bow enclosing a splat-like arrangement of lesser bows, with a turned spindle in the central position, was probably always a rarity,[47] in the same way as would have been the recurved-bow of an eccentric English Windsor mentioned in Chapter III, Section VI. If the system of dating employed by certain American authorities is soundly based, bow-back Windsors were known in America by the second or third quarter of the eighteenth century; but it seems fairly evident that few surviving examples there ante-date the end of the eighteenth century, when they are not obviously of later period. Nor, again as in England, is there any cause to suggest that the comb-back Windsor was sharply ousted by the bow-back, the one continuing to be made alongside the other for at any rate a perceptible period. Some chairs and settees have the slight carving popularly known as 'fingers' on the knuckles of the arms.

In America, too, the advent of the nineteenth century is a rough-and-ready signpost to radical changes of taste. It is about this period that one becomes conscious of the so-called 'rod-back' Windsors of a type attributed to 'Sheraton' influence, in which the comb or bow is dispensed with, the back being filled with vertical sticks between splayed uprights and crowned by a narrow top-rail. Chairs of this sort which present the typically nineteenth-century feature of a secondary rail closely below the top-rail, the intervening space being filled by a continuation of the back-sticks or by small inserted spindles, have been nicknamed 'dovecote' or 'pigeonhole' chairs.[48] This feature sometimes, though far from always, occurs on the early nineteenth-century type called 'Arrow-back', so styled from the shape of its flattened back-rails, slowly swelling from a relatively narrow base and suddenly sharpened to a point at the upper end. In fact, these rails are not 'arrows' at all, but a severely simplified form of a vase-shaped rail such as is seen in Sheraton's *Cabinet-Maker and Upholsterer's Drawing Book* (1791-4). A willing eye may trace a vague analogy between these 'arrows' and the very unusual English splat mentioned in Chapter III, Section VI, and again in the narrower, rounded rails, with a low-placed swell, in the backs of certain Wycombe Windsors of approximately mid-nineteenth-century period.

Single chairs might have, say, four such rails, but an early nineteenth-century Rocking-Chair in the Metropolitan Museum, New York, has the main part of its back filled with three moderately substantial examples, thus in some wise approximating to the triple-splat system as noticed in Chapter III. This chair is completed by a superimposed head-rest of traditional 'comb' type, a detail which, however grateful and comforting, somewhat destroys its proportions. This arrow-back, however, is a late development of the American Windsor Rocker, more traditional examples being of one or another form of stick-back.[49]

IV

On the claim that a certain English firm, Benjamin North of West Wycombe, produced the 'first' American Rocking-Chair, I have written in an earlier book.[50] Suffice to say here that I found no cause to accept it, though the enormous export of chairs from the Wycombe district may well have included 'Rockers'. The Rocker, in its various forms, including Windsor types, has been well known on both sides of the herring-pond for quite a while, though, so far as popularity alone is concerned, I hazard the guess that Rockers were rather less suited to English than to American taste. In America, the invention of the Rocking Chair has been attributed to none less than Benjamin Franklin, though this may be one of those cases of independent discovery which crop up every now and again in the arts and crafts. Quite old (non-Windsor) Rocking Chairs are occasionally found in England, where the application of runners to cradles—and children's rocking-horses—is respectably ancient. Of some of the chairs, it is at least probable that the runners were added at a later date, and this equally applies to certain American Windsors. Without dogmatizing, or necessarily excluding earlier examples, it can be said that the *main* period of the Rocking-Chair *made as such* was the nineteenth century, and that applies to both countries. As for the rest, some chairs were Rockers, some have lost their runners, and some have had rockerdom thrust upon them. A shortened leg may, just conceivably, indicate a chair shorn of its runners, though in England it more likely denotes an ordinary chair cut down for use as a Nursing Chair, or one of which the lower ends of the legs had been broken, or rotted by standing on a damp or well-washed floor. That a wastage of Rockers must be allowed for is the less deplorable in view of the fact that relatively few such Windsors seem to have possessed any outstanding quality of design. Merely to mount so essentially static an article as a chair on runners which lend it a certain, if limited, dynamic function, is to provoke a visual unease. Only such Rockers as are designed throughout in a mood of partial mobility can be aesthetically successful at all points.

Stylistically, some of the most successful American rockers of Windsor vintage were of 'arrow-head' type, though not all examples are of pleasing proportions. As much may be said of their 'successors' (if that term be permissible in the case of what was doubtless a gradual replacement), the vaunted 'Boston Rockers' which began their long career, with an almost ironic appropriateness, about the time that the old and by now imbecile King George III died at the original Windsor in England. With the Boston Rocker is reached the *terminus ad quem* of old American Windsors.[51] It remained in high favour for so many decades that the latest examples are more secondhand than antique; but, though this fact has displeased fastidious collectors, the Boston Rocker is not a type that can be ignored. If (as a Windsor) undeniably decadent, this popular chair with its distinctive 'roll' seat (replacing the older, characteristic saddle), its rolled arms, and heavily crested stick-back, was not only comfortable but, in its earlier phases, achieved a certain standard of grace. Its position in American Windsordom is roughly analogous to that of English stick- or lath-back Windsors of equivalent period.

V

However reasonable it may be to regard English and American Windsors as the cousins they doubtless were, each showed distinctions as well as similarities—as cousins are apt to do. Allowing that English Windsors were reaching America well back in the eighteenth century, and that the supply of old Colonial and Federal examples has been reinforced in modern times by the importation of genuine antiques of English origin, it is both possible and, in the more obvious cases, easy to distinguish the national temper of an American Windsor from that of its English counter-part. Easy, that is, when one has seen enough of both, whether in being or in photographs, to detect not only differences of construction or detail, but that imponderable element which is the silent voice of nationhood.

On a question sometimes posed—did the finest Windsors come from England or America?—I leave the decision to the reader's common sense. Beyond dispute, very fine chairs were produced in America, but occasional attempts to depreciate English Windsors as graceless, clumsy, or what-ever be the chosen derogation, can only be based on an imperfect acquain-tance with English work at its best, and even at less than its best; and in the matter of the worst neither nation has anything to boast about. Windsors of excellent quality have been made in England; Windsors of excellent quality have been made in America. Decent, friendly, common-place-pieces have been made in both; as have some quite deplorably bad in design. One can but pick and choose according to one's needs, one's luck, and the depth of one's pocket, always bearing in mind that the connoisseur, to whom quality is paramount, may choose differently from the antiquary or student primarily concerned with other, equally valid, considerations; and differently again from the 'small collector' mainly interested in furnishing a modest home.

What clearly emerges is that of all traditional types of chair, the Windsor is among the most interesting, sightly, and usable, and one in which, despite the march of centuries, there yet exists the breath of life.

APPENDIX

Loudon on Windsors

Of ACCOUNTS of the manufacture of English Windsors, a particular interest attaches to that in *An Encyclopædia of Cottage, Farm, and Villa Architecture and Furniture*, by John Claudius Loudon, F.L.S. (1783-1843), landscape gardener and writer, mainly on horticultural subjects. Originally published in 1833, his *Encyclopædia* was re-issued more than once, notably in 1842 and 1857, the last-named edition, revised by his widow, having a preface dated from Bayswater in April 1846. In all three editions, the description of Windsors is identical.

The value of Loudon's account of the making of Windsors centres in the fact that he gathered his material before the introduction of modern methods of machine-production. It typifies conditions obtaining in the early 1830's, and though too limited in scope to give a complete picture of Windsor chairmaking, is nevertheless informative.

Judging from his text and wood-engravings (not here reproduced), Loudon did not know, or did not attempt to cover, every type of Windsor then in use. To him, a Windsor was a bow-back with sticks and perforated splat of debased design, a simple dished seat, and turned legs and stretchers. He did not realize that Scroll Chairs (see Chapter III, Section 11) were also Windsors, though he noted that their seats (and underframing) were 'like the Windsor pattern'. On this minor point, we can correct Loudon, as Scroll Windsors are clearly, and by common consent, of the Windsor *genus*; but his account, especially of the staining process, is well worth repetition.

The following quotation from pp. 319-320 of the *Encyclopædia* is slightly abridged by the omission of most of the figure-references.

'639 *Kitchen Chairs.* Fig 643 is a Windsor Chair, one of the best kitchen chairs in general use in the midland counties of England. The seat is of elm, somewhat hollowed out; the outer rail [bow] of the back is of ash, in one piece, bent to the sort of horseshoe form shown, by being previously heated or steamed; its ends are then inserted in two holes bored through the seat, and are wedged firmly in from the underside. An additional support is given to the back, by two round rails [sticks], which are also made fast in two holes, formed in a projecting part of the seat. These chairs are sometimes painted, but more frequently stained with diluted sulphuric acid and logwood; or by repeatedly washing them over with alum water, which has some tartar in it; they should afterwards be washed over several times with an extract of Brasil wood. The colour given will be a sort of red, not unlike that of mahogany; and, by afterwards oiling the chair and rubbing it well, and for a long time, with woollen cloths, the veins and shading of the elm will be rendered conspicuous. Quicklime slacked in urine, and laid on the wood while hot, will also stain it of a red colour; and this is said to be the general practice with the Windsor chair manufacturers in the neighbourhood of London'.

(This may be compared with an account given to me by Alderman R. A. Janes, which describes how the Staining Boy dipped chairs into a large copper of boiling stain coloured with Logwood or Copperas. When a golden yellow-tone was desired, all parts except the seat were stained with Aquafortis, applied by rags tied on to sticks.)

Loudon next introduces a typical Scroll Windsor of plain design as 'a chair with a seat like the Windsor pattern, but with a different back, the two side styles [uprights] of which are mortised into the seat. The legs are put together by dowels (wedges put in tenons after they are inserted in the mortise, to prevent them [the legs] from being drawn back), like the Windsor chairs before mentioned. This forms a very comfortable and cheap chair'.

On general grounds, Loudon's *Encyclopædia* deserves to be better known to students of nineteenth-century furniture.

Notes

[1] William Gaunt: *The Pre-Raphaelite Tragedy* (London: Jonathan Cape 1942; ed. 1948), p. 201.

[2] Arthur Hayden: *Chats on Cottage and Farmhouse Furniture*, edited and revised by Cyril G. E. Bunt (London: Ernest Benn Ltd, ed. 1950), p. 167.

[3] Distinct from the Royal House of Windsor, which assumed Windsor as its surname in 1917.

[4] Sir Lawrence Weaver: *High Wycombe Furniture* (London: The Fanfare Press, 1929), p. 26.

[5] For a good rendering of such corner-chairs as these in their proper setting, see a drawing of an interior at *Schloss Enn, Tyrol*, by Tony Grubhofer, repr. *The Studio*, Vol. V, 1895, p. 9.

[6] R. W. Symonds: English Furniture from Charles II to George II. (The Connoisseur, 1929), p. 79.

[7] F. Gordon Roe: *English Cottage Furniture* (Phoenix House Ltd, 1949; 2nd impression, 1950), *passim*.

[8] Articles other than chairs, settees, and stools were made in the Windsor technique, but this book is concerned with seating.

[9] *Repr.* Ralph Edwards, F.S.A.: *A History of the English Chair* (H.M. Stationery Office, 1951), pl. 80.

[10] Therle Hughes: *Old English Furniture* (Lutterworth Press, 1949), p. 96.

[11] Anon: *The Windsor Chair Maker's Tools* (*n.d.*, a brief but useful pamphlet to which the curious reader is referred for further details).

[12] Weaver: *op. cit.*, p. 17. Dean, Chilton, & Smith are surnames of bodgers mentioned by Weaver. See also Roe: *English Cottage Furniture*, p. 58.

[13] Weaver: *op. cit.*, pp. 17-18.

[14] Weaver, *op. cit.*, p. 18. The wood thus bought was known as a 'fall of timber' (Alderman R. A. Janes). For further information *re* bodgers, Miss K. S. Wood's *Rural Crafts of England* (London: George G. Harrap & Co Ltd, 1949), can be consulted.

[15] Weaver, *op. cit.*, p. 17.

[16] Weaver: *op. cit.*, p. 11. Their names are among those recorded on the central or Wycombe window, unveiled October, 1911. 'Samuel

Treacher and Thomas Widgington appear to have been our earliest chair manufacturers, the former at Bowdrey's-lane and the latter at St. Mary-street. They were both in business soon after 1800, Mr Treacher having been born in 1769 and Mr Widgington in 1772. There is a record of a fire having taken place at Widgington's Chair Factory in 1810, and there is in existence a stained glass panel advertising Samuel Treacher's chairs, in 1832, . . . '(*Memorial Windows at the Town Hall, High Wycombe, Bucks,* October, 1911.)

[17] One 'Bonaventur Wygynton' was baptized at Great Marlow, 18 February, 1598; and a 'Thomas wigington', son of 'George wigington', 22 September, 1605. (Alfred Heneage Cocks, M.A., F.S.A.: *The Earliest Register of the Parish of Great Marlow, Buckinghamshire,* 1592-1611. (Exeter: William Pollard & Co, 1904).) I am advised by the Vicar of Great Marlow (the Rev D. J. Amies, R.D.) that there is no baptismal entry under the name Widgington in the years 1768-1775 inclusive; though a Thomas, son of James and Mary Wiginton, was baptized there, 6 August, 1775. Mr Amies has further courteously informed me that he knows of no one in Great Marlow now named Widgington, nor does he ever hear the name. Be it added that there is no patent difficulty in the variation of spelling as between Wiginton, Wigington, and Widgington.

[18] W. P. W. Phillimore, M.A., B.C.L., & Thomas Gurney: *Buckinghamshire Parish Registers (Marriages).* VI (1910) p. 118. Henry Kingston: *The History of Wycombe* (High Wycombe: Charles Foyster (1848) p. 111), mentions 'the house of the late Mr Samuel Treacher on the north side of the street of Wycombe leading towards Oxford'.

[19] High Wycombe Public Library, 794.31 L.50,099.

[20] *Ibid.,* 749.31. L.50,100.

[21] *Ibid.,* 749.31. L.50,051. A more perfect copy, with price-list inserted, is still with the firm of Thomas Glenister Ltd, Temple Works, High Wycombe, which also owns a number of its illustrated broadsheets of later date, all of which I have courteously been enabled to examine.

[22] *Bucks Free Press,* 20 January, 1950. Yet another instance is a modern Gothick Windsor in the London Library, presented by members in 1951 to commemorate service of Mr F. C. Fallon, Library Assistant 1914-50.

[23] For this date as for some other personalia, I am indebted to Goodchild's widow, Mrs (Elizabeth) Goodchild, who kindly verified some details for me. The name Goodchild is of frequent occurrence in the Chilterns, where it is sometimes pronounced 'Goo'ch'll'. The name

appears on the historic return of defaulters from Ship Money (headed by the illustrious John Hampden) at Great Kimble, 1635-6. I could not gather from 'Jack' Goodchild himself that he had any traditional knowledge of this circumstance. No mention of the name occurs among those of chairmakers at Naphill in *A Local Guide and Directory for the Town of High Wycombe* (preface dated July, 1875), though Edwin Goodchild is noted as a chair manufacturer in High Wycombe itself (Slater Street, North Town). An inquiry to Mrs 'Jack' Goodchild, as to whether this Edwin Goodchild was of 'Jack's' kin, proved fruitless, though she had asked 'an old man over 90 who once worked for her husband, and had known his grandfather'.

24 R. W. Symonds: *English Cane Chairs*, in *The Connoisseur* (March and May, 1951).

25 R. W. Symonds in *Apollo*, August, 1935, p. 69.

26 Ralph Edwards, F.S.A.: *A History of the English Chair* (H.M. Stationery Office, 1951), p. 27, pl. 78.

27 Therle Hughes: *Old English Furniture*, p. 95.

28 *Repr.* Ralph Edwards, F.S.A. *op. cit.* (1951), pl. 80.

29 For a careful reproduction in colour of this plate, see *The Connoisseur*, February, 1916, p. 85.

30 *Repr.* Ralph Edwards, F.S.A.: *op. cit.*, pl. 99.

31 This chair is assigned by Macquoid and Edwards to *circa* 1770, an estimation which I note without committing myself to it.

32 *Frederick Augustus, Duke of York and Albany*, K.G., by Sir David Wilkie, R.A., dated 1823, in the National Portrait Gallery, London.

33 Still more recent repetitions of the 'Goldsmith' type are also in evidence.

34 For the Cotswold type, see J. D. U. Ward in *Antiques* (1935). He mentions the 'elaborately shaped seat' as a feature.

35 Symonds, in *Apollo*, November, 1935, p. 266.

36 *Ibid.*

37 Edward Stratton Holloway: *American Furniture and Decoration, Colonial and Federal*. (New York and London: J. B. Lippincott & Co., 1928), p. 57.

38 Chair belonging to the American Philosophical Society, Philadelphia. For a critical estimate of the date of this historic chair and its subsequent alterations, see Thomas Hamilton Ormsbee: *The Story of American Furniture* (New York: Macmillan Co, ed. 1946), pp. 195, 219.

39 Portrait in Yale University Art Gallery. *Repr.* Charles Nagel: *American Furniture, 1650-1850*, (London: Max Parrish & Co, 1949), pl. 34.

[40] Carl Bridenbaugh: *The Colonial Craftsman*. (New York University Press, and Oxford University Press, 1950), p. 143.

[41] John C. Fitzpatrick: *The Writings of George Washington* (Washington: United States Government Printing Office, 1931), Vol. II, p. 138. Douglas Southall Freeman: *George Washington: A Biography*. (London: Eyre & Spottiswoode, 1947), Vol. II, p. 265.

[42] Carl Bridenbaugh: *op. cit.*, p. 77.

[43] Thomas Hamilton Ormsbee: *The Story of American Furniture*. (New York: Macmillan Co, ed. 1946), p. 197.

[44] Chair formerly in the collection of that keen, if eccentric, collector Cummings E. Davis (*ob.* 1896), now belonging to the Concord Antiquarian Society. *Repr.* Russell H. Kettell: *Cummings E. Davis and the Concord Antiquarian Society*, in the magazine *Antiques*. (New York), Vol. LVIII, August, 1950, No. 2, p. 109.

[45] Thomas Hamilton Ormsbee: *The Story of American Furniture*, p. 210.

[46] Note, however, the 'arrow-head' rocker described on page 78.

[47] Wallace Nutting: *Furniture Treasury*. (New York: Macmillan Co, 1948). Fig. 2671. Also *A Windsor Handbook*. (Framingham and Boston: Old America Co., 1917.)

[48] Wallace Nutting: *Furniture Treasury*, Figs. 2684, 2702.

[49] For illustrations of examples see (*inter al.*) Ormsbee: *op. cit.*; Frances Clary Morse: *Furniture of the Olden Time*. (New York: Macmillan Co, ed., 1946).

[50] F. Gordon Roe: *Victorian Furniture* (London: Phoenix House Ltd), pp. 62-63.

[51] For examples see (*inter al.*) Wallace Nutting: *Furniture Treasury*, Fig. 2467; Thomas Hamilton Ormsbee: *The Story of American Furniture*, Fig. 79; Frances Clary Morse: *Furniture of the Olden Time*, Fig. 150.

Short Bibliography

Indicates American Windsors

ANON.—*A Valuation of the Houses, Gardens, Farms, Lands, Mills, etc. in the Parish of Chepping Wycombe, Bucks.* (MS., 1837), High Wycombe Public Library.

—— *A Local Guide and Directory for the Town of High Wycombe.* (High Wycombe: William Judson, preface dated July, 1875.)

—— *High Wycombe Illustrated, Its Resources and Advantages.* (London: Tyer & Abbott, n.d. [late nineteenth century].)

—— *Memorial Windows at the Town Hall, High Wycombe, Bucks.* (Pamphlet, October, 1911).

—— *The Windsor Chair Maker's Tools: A Descriptive Guide to the Collection in the High Wycombe Museum.* (High Wycombe: Hague & Gill, n.d. [1948].)

—— *Unique Exhibition of Windsor Chairs* (at High Wycombe Museum). (Report in *Bucks Free Press*, 10 September, 1948.)

—— *M.P.s see Furniture in the Making.* (Report in *Bucks Free Press*, 9 July, 1948.)

—— *Craftsman Dies* [H. E. Goodchild]. (Obituary in *Bucks Free Press*, 8 December, 1950; correspondence by Dennis Young and F. Gordon Roe, 5 January, 1951.)

*Antiques. The Magazine (New York: various issues.)

B.N. [Benjamin North; West Wycombe]: See *Pattern Books.*

**HAROLD LEWIS BOND: *An Encyclopedia of Antiques.* (New York, Tudor Publishing Co., 1947.)

**CARL BRIDENBAUGH: *The Colonial Craftsman.* (New York University Press and Oxford University Press, 1950.)

CYRIL G. E. BUNT: see *Arthur Hayden.*

ADRIAN BURY, Hon. R. W. S.: *Mr Goodchild's Immortal Chairs.* (Article in *Everybody's*, 2 October, 1948, pp. 14-15.)

RALPH EDWARDS, F.S.A.: *Victoria and Albert Museum—Catalogue of English Furniture and Woodwork.* Vol. IV, *Georgian.* (London: H.M. Stationery Office, 1931.)

Victoria and Albert Museum—A History of the English Chair. (H.M. Stationery Office, 1951.) (See also *Macquoid and Edwards.*)

*JOHN C[LEMENT] FITZPATRICK: *The Writings of George Washington*, Vol. II. (Washington: United States Government Printing Office, 1931.)

*DOUGLAS SOUTHALL FREEMAN: *George Washington: A Biography*, Vol. II. (London: Eyre & Spottiswoode, 1949.)

GLENISTER & GIBBONS: See *Pattern Books*.

JOHN GLOAG: *English Furniture*. (London: Adam & Charles Black, 2nd ed., 1946.)
A Short Dictionary of Furniture. (London, Allen & Unwin, 1952.)

M. HARRIS & SONS: *The English Chair: Its History and Evolution*. (London: 1946.)

ARTHUR HAYDEN: *Chats on Cottage and Farmhouse Furniture*, ed. & rev. by Cyril G. E. Bunt. (London: Ernest Benn Ltd, ed. 1950.)

THERLE HUGHES: *Old English Furniture*. (London: Lutterworth Press, 1949.)

R. A. JANES: *Wycombe Memories*. (Article in *The Cabinet Maker and Complete House Furnisher*, No. 2702, 4 August, 1951, pp. 421-423.)

MARGARET JOURDAIN: see *John C. Rogers*.

*JOE KINDIG III: *Upholstered Windsors*. (Article in *Antiques*, July 1952, pp. 52-3.)

HENRY KINGSTON: *The History of Wycombe; with Recollections of My Native Town*. (High Wycombe: Charles Foyster, preface dated October, 1848.)

J. C. LOUDON, F.L.S.: *An Encyclopædia of Cottage, Farm, and Villa Architecture and Furniture*. (London: Longman, Rees, Orme, Brown, Green, & Longman, 1833.)

PERCY MACQUOID, R.I., and RALPH EDWARDS, F.S.A.: *The Dictionary of English Furniture*. (London: Country Life Ltd, Vol. 1, 1924.)

*N. HUDSON MOORE: *The Collector's Manual*. (New York: Tudor Publishing Co, ed. 1946.)

*FRANCES CLARY MORSE: *Furniture of the Olden Time*. (New York: Macmillan Co, ed. 1946.)

*CHARLES NAGEL: *American Furniture 1650-1850*. (London: Max Parrish & Co Ltd, 1949.)

*WALLACE NUTTING: *A Windsor Handbook*. (Framingham and Boston: Old America Co., 1917.) *Furniture Treasury*. (New York: Macmillan Co, Vol. 11, ed. 1948.)

*THOMAS HAMILTON ORMSBEE: *The Story of American Furniture.* (New York: Macmillan Co, ed. 1946.)

PATTERN BOOKS.

—— B.N. [? Benjamin North, West Wycombe]: *Antique and Plain and Ornamental Chairs.* (n.d., c. 1860's). High Wycombe Public Library.

—— Thomas Glenister: *[Chair Designs].* (Book of Water-Colour drawings, with some in pencil.) (? 3rd quarter of nineteenth century.) Thomas Glenister Ltd, High Wycombe.

—— Various illustrated Trade Catalogues and broadsheets. (Late nineteenth century.)

—— Glenister & Gibbons: *Patterns of Cane, Windsor, Fancy and Other Chairs.* (n.d., c. 1865-79.) Thomas Glenister Ltd, High Wycombe: a less perfect copy is in High Wycombe Public Library.

F. GORDON ROE, F.S.A.: *English Cottage Furniture.* (London: Phoenix House Ltd, 1949; 2nd ed. 1950.)

—— *Victorian Furniture.* (Phoenix House Ltd, 1952.)

JOHN C. ROGERS, A.R.I.B.A.: *English Furniture,* rev. and enlarged by Margaret Jourdain. (London: Country Life Ltd, ed. 1950.)

JAMES JOSEPH SHEAHAN: *History and Topography of Buckinghamshire.* (London: Longman, Green, Longman & Roberts, 1862.)

EDWIN SKULL: Large illustrated Broadsheet for 'Edwin Skull, Manufacturer of Every Description of Chairs, High Wycombe, Bucks. No connection with any other house'. (*Post* October, 1865.) High Wycombe Public Library.

WALTER SKULL: *Chair Designs.* (Book of water-colour drawings, with inserted modern titlepage) (1849). High Wycombe Public Library.

C. F. F. SNOW: *Chairs from the Chilterns.* (H. E. Goodchild.) (Article in *Country Life,* 6 February, 1942, pp. 250-1.)

*DAVID STOCKWELL: *Windsors in Independence Hall.* (Article in *Antiques,* September, 1952 pp. 214-15.)

R. W. SYMONDS: *The Windsor Chair.* (Articles in *Apollo,* August and November, 1935.)

J. D. U. WARD: *English Windsor Chairs* (In *Antiques,* December, 1935, pp. 234-7.)

—— *Making English Windsors: A Pictorial Demonstration.* [H. E. Goodchild.] (In *Antiques,* September, 1950, pp. 190-1.)

Sir LAWRENCE WEAVER, K.B.E., F.S.A., Hon. A.R.I.B.A.: *High Wycombe Furniture*. (London: The Fanfare Press, 1929.)

K. S. WOODS: *Rural Crafts of England*. (London: George G. Harrap & Co Ltd, 1949.) (Includes bodgers.)

INDEX